# A POPULAR SCHOOLGIRL

ANGELA BRAZIL

1st WORLD
LIBRARY
Literary Society

# A Popular Schoolgirl

## Angela Brazil

© 1st World Library, 2006
PO Box 2211
Fairfield, IA 52556
www.1stworldlibrary.com
First Edition

LCCN: 2006907698

Softcover ISBN: 1-4218-2416-7
Hardcover ISBN: 1-4218-2316-0
eBook ISBN: 1-4218-2516-3

Purchase *"A Popular Schoolgirl"*
as a traditional bound book at:
www.1stWorldLibrary.com/purchase.asp?ISBN=1-4218-2416-7

1st World Library is a literary, educational organization
dedicated to:

- Creating a free internet library of downloadable ebooks

  - Hosting writing competitions and offering book
    publishing scholarships.

---

**Interested in more 1st World Library books?**
contact: literacy@1stworldlibrary.com
**Check us out at: www.1stworldlibrary.com**

# 1ˢᵗ World Library Literary Society

## Giving Back to the World

"If you want to work on the core problem, it's early school literacy."

**- James Barksdale, former CEO of Netscape**

"No skill is more crucial to the future of a child, or to a democratic and prosperous society, than literacy."

**- Los Angeles Times**

Literacy... means far more than learning how to read and write... The aim is to transmit... knowledge and promote social participation."

**- UNESCO**

"Literacy is not a luxury, it is a right and a responsibility. If our world is to meet the challenges of the twenty-first century we must harness the energy and creativity of all our citizens."

**- President Bill Clinton**

"Parents should be encouraged to read to their children, and teachers should be equipped with all available techniques for teaching literacy, so the varying needs and capacities of individual kids can be taken into account."

**- Hugh Mackay**

# CONTENTS

I. THE END OF THE HOLIDAYS ......................................... 7

II. OPENING DAY ............................................................. 17

III. WYNCH-ON-THE-WOLD ............................................. 26

IV. INTRUDER BESS .......................................................... 36

V. THE FIFTH-FORM FETE ................................................ 45

VI. THE SCHOOL PARLIAMENT ........................................ 57

VII. HOCKEY ..................................................................... 67

VIII. AN UNPLEASANT EXPERIENCE ............................... 76

IX. A HOSTEL FROLIC........................................................ 89

X. THE WHISPERING STONES ......................................... 100

XI. ON STRIKE ................................................................. 111

XII. THE RAINBOW LEAGUE ,,,.......... ............................ 123

XIII. QUENREDE COMES OUT......................................... 133

XIV. THE PEEP-HOLE....................................................... 143

XV. BROTHERLY BREEZES................................................ 152

XVI. AN EASTER PILGRIMAGE ........................................ 164

XVII. THE RIVALS .............................................................. 172

XVIII. BESS AT HOME ........................................................ 185

XIX. THE NUN'S WALK...................................................... 192

XX. UNDER THE LANTERNS ............................................ 204

XXI. THE ABBEY RECITAL................................................. 213

# CHAPTER I

## THE END OF THE HOLIDAYS

"Ingred! Ingred, old girl! I say, Ingred! Wherever have you taken yourself off to?" shouted a boyish voice, as its owner, jumping an obstructing gooseberry bush, tore around the corner of the house from the kitchen garden on to the strip of rough lawn that faced the windows. "Hullo! Cuckoo! Coo-ee! *In*-gred!"

"I'm here all the time, so you needn't bawl!" came in resigned tones from under the shade of a large fuchsia. "You're enough to wake the dead, Chumps! What is it you want now! It's too hot to go a walk till after tea. I'm trying to get ten minutes peace and quiet!"

Hereward, otherwise "Chumps," put his feet together in the second position, flung out his arms in what was intended to be a graceful attitude, and made a mock bow worthy of the cinema stage.

"Have them by all means, Madam!" he replied in mincing accents. "Your humble servant has no wish to disturb your ladyship's elegant repose. He offers a thousand apologies for his unceremonious entrance into your august presence, and implores you to condescend - *Ow! Stop it, you brute!*"

Hereward's burst of eloquence was brought to an abrupt end by the violent onslaught of a fox-terrier puppy which flung itself upon him and began to worry his ankles with delighted yelps of appreciation.

"Stop it! Keep off, I tell you! I *won't* be chewed to ribbons!" he protested, dodging the attacks of the playful but all too sharp teeth, and catching the little dog by the piece of tarred rope that formed its collar. "Here, you'll get throttled in a minute if you don't mend your manners."

"Give him to his auntie, bless his heart!" laughed Ingred, extending welcoming arms to the fat specimen of puppyhood, and rolling him about on her knee. "Oh, he *did* make you dance! You looked so funny! There, precious! Don't chump auntie's fingers. Go bye-byes now. Snuggle down on auntie's dress, and -"

"If you've *quite* finished talking idiotic nonsense to that little beast," interrupted Hereward sarcastically, "you'll perhaps kindly oblige me by mentioning whether you're coming or not!"

"Not coming anywhere - too hot!" grunted Ingred, resettling her cushion under the fuchsia bush.

"Right you are! Please yourself and you'll please me! Though I should have thought the run to Chatcombe -"

Ingred sprang to her feet, dropping the puppy unceremoniously.

"You don't mean to say Egbert's finished mending the motor bike? You abominable boy! Why couldn't you tell me so before?"

"You never gave me the chance - just said off-hand you wouldn't go anywhere. Yes, the engine's running like a daisy, and the sidecar's on, and Egbert's fussing to be off. If you really change your mind and want to go -"

But by this time Ingred was round the corner of the house; so, shaking a philosophic head at the ways of girls in general, her brother gathered a gooseberry or two en route, and followed her in the direction of the stable-yard.

The Saxons were spending their summer holidays at a farm near the seaside, and for the first time in four long years the whole family was reunited. Mr. Saxon, Egbert, and Athelstane had only just been demobilized, and had hardly yet settled down to civilian life. They had joined the rest of the party at Lynstones before returning to their native town of Grovebury. The six weeks by the sea seemed a kind of oasis between the anxious period of the war that was past and gone, and the new epoch that stretched ahead in the future. To Ingred they were halcyon days. To have her father and brothers safely back, and for the family to be together in the midst of such beautiful scenery, was sufficient for utter enjoyment. She did not wish her mind to venture outside the charmed circle of the holidays. Beyond, when she thought about it all, lay a nebulous prospect, in the center of which school loomed large.

On this particular hot August afternoon, Ingred welcomed an excursion in the sidecar. She had not felt inclined to walk down the white path under the blazing sun to the glaring beach, but it was another matter to spin along the high road till, as the fairy tales put it, her hair whistled in the wind. Egbert was anxious to set off, so Hereward took his place on the luggage-carrier, and, after some back-firing, the three started forth. It was a glorious run over moorland country, with glimpses of the sea on the one hand, and craggy tors on the other, and round them billowy masses of heather, broken here and there by runnels of peat-stained water. If Egbert exceeded the speed-limit, he certainly had the excuse of a clear road before him; there were no hedges to hide advancing cars, neither was there any possibility of whisking round a corner to find a hay-cart blocking the way. In the course of an hour they had covered a considerable number of miles, and found themselves whirling down the tremendous hill that led to the seaside town of Chatcombe.

Arrived in the main street they left the motorcycle at a garage, and strolled on to the promenade, joining the crowd of holiday-makers who were sauntering along in the heat, or sitting on the benches watching the children digging in the sand below. Much to Ingred's astonishment she was suddenly hailed by her name, and, turning, found herself greeted with enthusiasm by a schoolfellow.

"Ingred! What a surprise!"

"Avis! Who'd have thought of seeing you?"

"Are you staying here?"

"No, only over for the afternoon."

"We've rooms at Beach View over there. Come along and have some tea with us, and your brothers too. Yes, indeed you must! Mother will be delighted to see you all. I shan't let you say no!"

Borne away by her hospitable friend, Ingred presently found herself sitting on a seat in the front garden of a tall boarding-house facing the sea, and while Egbert and Hereward discussed motor-cycling with Avis's father, the two girls enjoyed a confidential chat together.

"Only a few days now," sighed Avis, "then we've got to leave all this and go home. How long are you staying at Lynstones, Ingred?"

"A fortnight more, but don't talk of going home. I want the holidays to last forever!"

"So do I, but they won't. School begins on the twenty-first of September. It will be rather sport to go to the new buildings at last, won't it? By the by, now the war's over, and we've all got our own again, I suppose you're going back to Rotherwood, aren't you?"

"I suppose so, when it's ready."

"But surely the Red Cross cleared out ages ago, and the whole place has been done up? I saw the paperhangers there in June."

"Oh, yes!" Ingred's voice was a little strained.

"You'll be so glad to be living there again," continued Avis. "I always envied you that lovely house. You must have hated lending it as a hospital. I expect when you're back you'll be giving all sorts of delightful parties, won't you? At least that's what the girls at school were saying."

"It's rather early to make plans," temporized Ingred.

"Oh, of course! But Jess and Francie said you'd a gorgeous floor for dancing. I do think a fancy-dress dance is about the best fun on earth. The next time I get an invitation, I'm going as a Quaker maiden, in a gray dress and the duckiest little white cap. Don't you think it would suit me? With your dark hair you ought to be something Eastern. I can just imagine you acting hostess in a shimmery sort of white-and-gold costume. *Do* promise to wear white-and-gold!"

"All right," laughed Ingred.

"It's so delightful that the war's over, and we can begin to have parties again, like we used to do. Beatrice Jackson told me she should never forget that Carnival dance she went to at Rotherwood five years ago, and all the lanterns and fairy lamps. Some of the other girls talk about it yet. Hullo, that's the gong! Come indoors, and we'll have tea."

Ingred was very quiet as she went back in the sidecar that evening, though Hereward, sitting on the luggage-carrier, was in high spirits, and fired off jokes at her the whole time. The fact was she was thinking deeply. Certain problems, which she had hitherto cast carelessly away, now obtruded themselves so definitely that they must at last be faced. The process, albeit necessary, was not altogether a pleasant one.

To understand Ingred's perplexities we must give a brief account of the fortunes of her family up to the time this story begins. Mr. Saxon was an architect, who had made a good connection in the town of Grovebury. Here he had designed and built for himself a very beautiful house, and had liberally entertained his own and his children's friends. When war broke out, he had been amongst the first to volunteer for his country's service, and, as a further act of patriotism, he and his wife had decided to offer the use of "Rotherwood" for a Red Cross Hospital. The three boys were then at school, Egbert and Athelstane at Winchester, and Hereward at a preparatory school; so, storing the furniture, Mrs. Saxon moved into rooms with Quenrede and Ingred, who were attending the girls' college in Grovebury as day boarders. For the whole period of the war this arrangement had continued; Rotherwood was given over to the wounded soldiers, and Mrs. Saxon herself worked as one of their most devoted nurses.

In course of time Egbert and Athelstane had also joined the army, and with three of her menkind at the front, their mother had been more than ever glad to fill up at the hospital the hours when her girls were absent from her at school. Then came the Armistice, and the blessed knowledge that, though not yet home again, the dear ones were no longer in danger. By April the Red Cross had finished its work in Grovebury; the remaining patients regretfully departed, the wards were dismantled of their beds, and Rotherwood was handed back to its rightful owners.

Naturally it needed much renovation and decorating before it was again fit for a private residence, and paperers and painters had been busy there for many weeks. They had only just removed the ladders by the middle of July.

It was nearly August before Mr. Saxon, Egbert, and Athelstane were finally demobilized, and they had gone straight to Lynstones to join the rest of the family at the farmhouse

Angela Brazil

rooms. What was to happen after the delirious joy of the holiday was over, Ingred did not know. She had several times mentioned to her mother the prospect of their return to Rotherwood, but Mrs. Saxon had always evaded the subject, saying: "Wait till Daddy comes back!" and the welcoming of their three heroes had seemed a matter of such paramount importance that in comparison with it even the question of their beloved Rotherwood might stand aside.

The Saxons were a particularly united family, tremendously proud of one another, and interested in each other's doings. Their name bespoke their old English origin, which (except in the case of Ingred) was further vouched for by their blue eyes, fair skins, and flaxen hair. Egbert and Athelstane were strapping young fellows of six feet, and thirteen-year-old Hereward was taller already than Ingred. Quenrede, immensely proud of her quaint Saxon name, and not at all pleased that the family generally shortened it to Queenie, had just left school, and had turned up her long fair pigtail, put on a grown-up and rather condescending manner, powdered the tip of her classic little nose, and was extremely particular about the cut of her skirts and the fit of her suede shoes. It was a grievance to Quenrede that, as she expressed it, she had "missed the war." She had longed to go out to France and drive an ambulance, or to whirl over English roads on a motorcycle, buying up hay for the Government, or to assist in training horses, or to help in some other patriotic job of an equally interesting and exciting character.

"It's *too* bad that just when I'm old enough all the jolly things are closed to women!" she groused. "If Mother had only let me leave school a year ago, I'd at least have had three months' fun. Life's going to be very slow now. There's nothing sporty to do at all!"

Ingred, the youngest but one, and fifteen on her last birthday, was the only dark member of the fair Saxon family. At present she was not nearly so good-looking as pretty Quenrede; her mouth was a trifle heavy and her cheeks lacked color; but her eyes had depths that were not seen in her sister's, and her thick brown hair fell far below her waist. She would gladly have exchanged it for the lint-white locks of Hereward.

"Queenie was always chosen for a fairy at school plays," she grumbled, "and they never would have me, though her dresses would have come in for me so beautifully. I don't see why some fairies shouldn't have dark hair! And it was just as bad when we acted *The Merchant of Venice*. Miss Carter gave 'Portia' to Francie Hall, and made me take 'Jessica,' and Francie was a perfect stick, and spoilt the whole thing! Next time, I declare I'll bargain to wear a golden wig, and see what happens."

Ingred had been educated at Grovebury College since the morning when, a fat little person of five, she had taken her place in the Kindergarten. She and Quenrede had always been favorites in the school. In pre-war days they had been allowed to give delightful parties at Rotherwood to their form-mates, and though that had not been possible during the last five years, everybody knew that their beautiful home had been lent to the Red Cross, and admired their patriotism in thus giving it for the service of the nation. From Avis's remarks that afternoon it was evident that the girls at the college expected the Saxons to return immediately to Rotherwood, and were looking forward to being invited to entertainments there during the coming autumn and winter. Ingred had contrived to parry her friend's interested questions, but she felt the time had come when she must be prepared to give some definite answer to those who inquired about their future plans. She managed to catch her mother alone next morning for a quiet chat.

"Mumsie, dear," she began. "I've been wanting to ask you this - are we going back to Rotherwood after the holidays?"

Mrs. Saxon folded up her sewing, put her thimble and scissors away in her work-basket, and leaned her elbow on the arm of the garden seat as if prepared for conversation.

Angela Brazil

"And I've been wanting to talk to you about this, Ingred. Shall you be very disappointed when I tell you 'No'?"

"Oh, Muvvie!" Ingred's tone was agonized.

"It can't be helped, little woman! It can't indeed! I think you're old enough now to understand if I explain. You know this war has hit a great many people very hard. There has been a sort of general financial see-saw; some have made large fortunes, but others have lost them. We come in the latter list. When your father went out to France, he had to leave his profession to take care of itself, and other architects have stepped in and gained the commissions that used to come to his office. It may take him a long while to pull his connection together again, and the time of waiting will be one of much anxiety for him. Then, most of our investments, which used to pay such good dividends, are worth hardly anything now, and only bring us in a pittance compared with former years. Instead of being rich people, we shall have to be very careful indeed to make ends meet. To return to Rotherwood is utterly out of the question, and with the price of everything doubled and trebled, and our income in the inverse ratio, it is impossible to keep up so big an establishment nowadays."

"Where are we going to live, then?" asked Ingred in a strangled voice.

"At the bungalow that Daddy built on the moors. Fortunately the tenant was leaving, and we had not let it to any one else. In present circumstances it will suit us very well. Athelstane is to be entered in the medical school at Birkshaw; he can ride over every day on the motor-bicycle. We had hoped to send him to study in London, but that's only one of the many plans that have 'gane agley'."

"Are Hereward and I to go in to Grovebury every day?"

"Hereward can manage it all right, but I shall arrange for you to be a weekly boarder at the new hostel. You can come home from Friday to Monday. Now, don't cry about it, childie!" as a big tear splashed down Ingred's dress. "After all, we've much to be thankful for. If we had lost Father, or Egbert, or Athelstane out in France we might indeed grieve. So long as we have each other we've got the best thing in life, and we must all cling together as a family, and help one another on. Cheer up!"

"It will be simply h - h - h - hateful to go back to school this term, and not live at R - r - r - rotherwood!" sobbed Ingred.

Her mother patted the dark head that rested against her knee.

"Poor little woman! Remember it's just as hard for all the rest of us. We've each got a burden to carry at present. Suppose we see who can be pluckiest over it. We're fighting fortune now, instead of the Hun, and we must show her a brave face. Won't you march with the family regiment, and keep the colors flying?"

"I'll try," said Ingred, scrubbing her eyes with her pocket-handkerchief.

# CHAPTER II

## OPENING DAY

The Girls' College at Grovebury, under its able head-mistress, Miss Burd, had made itself quite a name in the neighborhood. The governors, realizing that it was outgrowing its old premises, decided to erect others, and had put up a handsome building in a good situation near the Abbey. No sooner was the last tile laid on the roof, however, than war broke out, and the new school was immediately commandeered by the Government as a recruiting office, and it had been kept for that purpose until after the Armistice.

The girls considered it a very great grievance to be obliged to remain cramped so long in their old college. The foundation stone of the new building had been laid by Queen Mary herself, and they thought the Government might have fixed upon some other spot in which to conduct business, instead of keeping them out of their proper quarters. All things come to an end, however, even the circumlocution and delays of Government offices, and by the beginning of the autumn term the removal had been effected, and the ceremony arranged for the opening of the new college. Naturally it was to be a great day. The Members of Parliament for Grovebury, and the Mayor, and many other important people were to be present, to say nothing of parents and visitors. The pupils, assembled in the freshly color-washed dressing-rooms, greeted one another excitedly.

"How do you like it?"

"Oh, it's topping!"

"Beats the old place hollow!"

"There's room to turn around here!"

"And the lockers are just A1."

"Have you seen the class-rooms?"

"Not yet."

"The gym's utterly perfect!"

"And so is the lab."

"Shame we've had to wait for it so long!"

"Never mind, we've got into it at last!"

Among the numbers of girls in the capacious dressing-rooms, Ingred also hung up her hat and coat, and passed on into the long corridor. Like the others she was excited, interested, even a little bewildered at the unfamiliar surroundings. It seemed extraordinary not to know her way about, and she seized joyfully upon Nora Clifford, who by virtue of ten minutes' experience could act cicerone.

"We're to be in VA.," Nora assured her. "All our old set, that is, except Connie Lord and Gladys Roper and Meg Mason. I've just met Miss Strong, and she told me. She's moved up with us, and there's a new mistress for VB. Haven't seen her yet, but they say she's nice, though I'd rather stick to Miss Strong, wouldn't you?"

"I don't know," temporized Ingred, screwing her mouth into a button.

"Oh, of course! I forgot! You're not a 'Strong' enthusiast - never were! Now *I* like her!"

"It's easy enough to like anybody who favors you. Miss Strong was always down on me somehow, and I'd rather have tried my luck with a fresh teacher. I wonder if Miss Burd would put me in VB. if I asked her."

"Of course she wouldn't! Don't be a silly idiot! I think Miss Strong's absolutely adorable. Don't you like the decorations in the corridor? Miss Godwin and some of the School of Art students did them. But just wait till you've seen the lecture-hall! Here we are! Now then, what d'you say to this?"

The big room into which Nora ushered her companion was lighted from the top, and the walls, distempered in buff, had been decorated with stencils of Egyptian designs, the bright barbaric colors of which gave a very striking effect. There was a platform at the far end, where were placed rows of chairs for the distinguished visitors, and also pots of palms and ferns and geraniums to add an air of festivity to the opening ceremony. The long lines of benches in the body of the hall were already beginning to fill with girls, their bright hair-ribbons looking almost like a further array of flowers. Mistresses here and there were ushering them to their places, the Kindergarten children to the front seats, Juniors to the middle, and Seniors to the rear. Ingred and Nora, motioned by Miss Giles to a bench about three-quarters down the room, took their seats and talked quietly with their nearest neighbors. A general buzz of conversation, constantly restrained by mistresses, kept rising and then falling again to subdued whispers. In a short time the hall was full, Miss Perry had opened the piano, and the choir leaders had ranged themselves round her. In dead silence all the girls, big and little, turned their eyes towards the platform. The door behind the row of palms and ferns was opening, and Miss Burd, in scholastic cap and gown, was ushering in the Mayor, the Mayoress, several Town Councilors and their wives, a few clergy, the head-master of the School of Art, and, to the place of honor in the middle, Sir James Hilton, the

Member of Parliament for Grovebury, who was to conduct the ceremony of the afternoon. He was a pleasant, genial-looking man, and though, as he assured his audience, he had never before had the opportunity of addressing a room full of girls, he seemed to be able to rise to the occasion, and made quite a capital speech.

"You're lucky to have this handsome building in which to do your lessons," he concluded. "Our environment makes a great difference to us, and I think it is far easier to turn out good work in the midst of beautiful surroundings. Grovebury College has reaped a well-deserved reputation in the past, and I trust that its hitherto excellent standards will be maintained or even surpassed in the future. As member for the town there's a special word I wish to say to you. Train yourselves to be good women citizens. Some day, when you're grown up, you will have votes, and in that way assist in the self-government of this great nation. The better educated and the more enlightened you are, the better fitted you will be for your civic responsibility. Every girl who does her duty at school is helping her country, because she is making herself efficient to serve it in some capacity. At present England stands at a great crisis; if we are to keep up the traditions of our forefathers we want workers, not slackers, in every department of life. Even the smallest of those little girls sitting in the front row can do her bit. As for you elder girls, think of yourselves as a Cadet Corps, training for the service of the British Empire, and let every lesson you learn be not for your own advantage, but for the good you can do with it afterwards to the world. I have very great pleasure in declaring this new building open."

After Sir James had sat down, the Mayor and several other people made short speeches, and when all the clapping had finally subsided, the piano struck up, and the school sang an Empire Song and the National Anthem. Then the door at the back of the platform opened again for the exit of the visitors, who, chatting among themselves, made their way to Miss Burd's study to be hospitably entertained with tea and cakes. The whole ceremony had barely occupied an hour, and it was

Angela Brazil

not yet four o'clock. The girls, in orderly files, marched from the lecture-hall, and betook themselves first to their new form-rooms, where textbooks were given out with preparation for the next day, and desks allotted; then, when the great bell rang for dismissal, to the playground and cloak-rooms, en route for home.

Ingred, with a goodly pile of fresh literature under her arm, walked slowly downstairs. She was not in any hurry to leave the class-room, and lingered as long as the limits of Miss Strong's patience lasted. She knew there was a certain ordeal to be faced with her form-mates, and she was not sure whether she wanted to put it off, or to get it over at once.

"Better let them know and have done with it," she said to herself after a few moments' consideration on the landing. "After all, it's my business, not theirs!"

It was a rather airily-defiant Ingred who strolled into the cloak-room and put on her hat. Francie Hall, trying to thread her boot with a lace that had lost its tag, looked up, smiled, and made room for her on the form.

"Cheery-ho, Ingred! How do you like our new diggings? Some removal, this, isn't it? I must say the place looks nice. It's topping to be here at last. By the by, I suppose you'll be getting in Rotherwood soon? Or have you got already?"

Ingred was stooping to lace her shoe, so perhaps the position accounted for her stifled voice.

"We're not going back there."

"Not going back!" Francie's tone was one of genuine amazement. "Why, but you said it was being done up for you, and you'd be moving before the term started!"

"Well, we're not, at any rate."

"What a disappointment for you!" began Beatrice Jackson tactlessly, as several other girls who were standing near turned and joined the group. "You always said you were just longing for Rotherwood."

"Do the Red Cross want it again?" queried Jess Howard.

"No, they don't; but we're not going to live there. Where are we going to live? At our bungalow on the moors, and I'm a weekly boarder at the hostel. Are there any other impertinent questions you'd like to ask? Don't all speak at once, please!"

And Ingred, having laced both shoes, got up, seized her pile of books, and, turning her back on her form-mates, stalked away without a good-by. She knew she had been rude and ungracious, but she felt that if she had stopped another moment the tears that were welling into her eyes would have overflowed. Ingred had many good points, but she was a remarkably proud girl. She could not bear her schoolfellows to think she had come down in the world. She had thrown out so many hints last term about the renewed glories of Rotherwood, that it was certainly humiliating to have to acknowledge that all the happy expectations had come to nothing. On the reputation of Rotherwood both she and Quenrede had held their heads high in the school; she wondered if her position would be the same, now that everybody knew the truth.

As a matter of fact, most of the girls giggled as she went out through the cloak-room door.

"My lady's in a temper!" exclaimed Francie.

"Lemons and vinegar!" hinnied Jess.

"Why did she fly out like that?" asked Beatrice.

"Well, really, Beatrice Jackson, after all the stupid things you said, anybody would fly out, I should think," commented Verity Richmond. "I'm sorry for Ingred. I'd heard the Saxons

Angela Brazil

can't go back to their old house. It's hard luck on them after lending it all these years to the Red Cross."

"But *why* aren't they going back?"

"Why, silly, because they can't keep it up, I suppose. If you've any sense, you won't mention Rotherwood to Ingred again. It's evidently a sore point. Don't for goodness sake, go rubbing it into her."

"I wasn't going to!" grumbled Beatrice. "Surely I can make an innocent remark without you beginning to preach to me like this! I call it cheek!"

Verity did not reply. She had had too many squabbles with Beatrice in the past to want to begin a fresh campaign on the first day of a new term. She discreetly pretended not to hear, and addressing Francie Hall, launched into an account of her doings during the holidays.

"We're moving out to Repworth at the September quarter," she concluded. "And it's too far for me to bicycle in to school every day, so I've started as a boarder at the hostel. I shall go home for week-ends, though. Nora Clifford and Fil Trevor are there too. They'll be glad Ingred's come. With four of us out of one form, things ought to be rather jinky. Hullo, here they are! I say, girls, let's go to our diggings."

The two girls who came strolling up arm-in-arm were the most absolute contrast. Nora was large-limbed, plump, rosy, with short-cut hair, a lively manner, and any amount of confidence. Without being exactly pretty, she gave a general impression of jolly, healthy girlhood, and reminded one of an old-fashioned, sweet-scented cabbage rose that had just burst into bloom. Dainty little Filomena might, on the other hand, be described as the most delicate of tea roses. She was fair to a fault, a lily-white maid with the silkiest of flaxen tresses. Her pale-blue eyes, with their light lashes, and rather colorless little face with its straight features were of the petite fairy type. You felt instinctively that, like a Dresden china vase, she was made more for ornament than for use, and nobody - even school-mistresses - expected too much from her. Experience had shown them that they did not get it.

For two years, ever since her mother's death, Fil had been a boarder at the College, and because at first she had been such a pathetic little figure in her deep mourning, the girls had petted her, and had continued an indulgent attitude long after the black dress had been exchanged for colors. If Fil had rather got into the habit of posing as the mascot of the form, she certainly deserved some consideration, for she was a dear little thing, with a very sweet temper, and never made any of the ill-natured remarks that some of the other girls flung about like missiles. She was so manifestly unfitted to take her own part that somebody else invariably took it for her.

Verity Richmond, who, with Nora, Filomena and Ingred, represented VA. in the hostel, was a brisk, up-to-date, go-ahead girl, full of fun and high spirits. She was a capital mimic, and had a turn for repartee that, quite good-naturedly, laid any adversary flat in the dust. If Nora and Fil were like rose and lily, she was decidedly the robin of the party. Her fair complexion seemed to add force to the brightness of her twinkling brown eyes, and her general restlessness and quick alert ways made one think of a bird always hopping about. Though not quite such a romp as Nora, she was ready for any fun that was going, and intended to get as much enjoyment as possible out of the coming term. She linked herself now on to Fil's disengaged arm, taking the latter's pile of books with her own and began towing her two friends in the direction of the hostel.

"I've hardly had time even for a squint at our dormitory yet," she announced. "Mrs. Best said I was late, and made me pop down my bag and fly; but she told me we were all four together, so I went off with an easy mind. I'd been worrying for fear I'd be boxed up with some kids, or sandwiched in among the Sixth. I told you Ingred was to be with us, didn't I?

Angela Brazil

Let's go and hunt her out; she'll have wiped her eyes and got over her jim-jams by now. We'll have time to do some unpacking before tea, if they've carried up our boxes."

The hostel was a separate house, built at the opposite side of the school playground. It could accommodate thirty girls, and twenty-six were already entered on its register. After a brief peep into the attractive dining-hall, and an equally pleasant-looking boarders' sitting-room, the three girls went upstairs to a dormitory marked 2. They found Ingred already at work on her task of unpacking, putting clothes away in drawers, and spreading the shelf that served as a dressing-table with an assortment of photos, books, and toilet requisites. She looked rather in the dumps, but it was impossible for anybody to remain gloomy when in the presence of such lively spirits as Nora and Verity, and by the time the gong sounded for tea she had cheered up, and was sitting on her bed discussing school news.

"Look here!" said Verity. "If we want to have a jolly term we four must stick together. Let's make a compact that, both in school and in the hostel, we'll support each other through thick and thin. We'll be a sort of society of Freemasons. I haven't made up any secrets yet, but whoever betrays them will be outlawed! Let's call ourselves 'The Foursome League.' Now then, put your right hands all together on mine, and say after me: 'I hereby promise and vow on my honor as a gentlewoman that I'll stand by my chums in No. 2 Dormitory at any cost.' That's a good beginning. When we've time, we'll draw up the rules. Subscriptions? Oh, bother! You can each give sixpence if you like, and we'll spend the money on a chocolate feast. Remember, Fil, not a word to anybody! It's to be kept absolutely quiet. There's the gong. If the tea's up to the standard of the rest of the hostel, I shan't object. Glad we're not rationed now, for I'm as hungry as a hunter."

# CHAPTER III

## WYNCH-ON-THE-WOLD

Though the College only opened on Tuesday afternoon, the short remainder of the week seemed enormously long to Ingred. Her form mates were the same, but everything else was absolutely changed; she might have been at a new school. She appreciated the convenient arrangements of the handsome building: the lecture-hall, with its stained-glass window and polished floor, the airy class-rooms, the studio with its facilities for every kind of art work, the three music-rooms, the laboratory, the gymnasium, and, last but not least, the hostel. Ingred had never before been a boarder, and she had not expected to like the experience, but there is a subtle charm in community life that infects everybody with "the spirit of the hive," and in spite of herself she began to be interested in the particular set of faces that met round the table for meals. The greater part of the girls were in the middle and lower school, but there were a few members of the Sixth, who sat next to Mrs. Best, the matron, and Nurse Warner, and looked with superior eyes on the crowd of intermediates and juniors. To have secured such congenial room-mates was an asset for which she could not be sufficiently thankful. Whatever troubles might await her downstairs, it was a comfort to know that she had three allies ready to flock to her support. She had not known any of them well in the past, but as they seemed prepared to offer their friendship, she also was ready to act the part of chum. By exchanging desks with Linda Slater, she managed to secure a seat next to Verity in school, and entered

Angela Brazil

into an arrangement with her that they should supply the missing gaps in each other's notes, for Miss Strong often lectured so rapidly that it was impossible to keep up with her.

"I wish I knew shorthand," grumbled Ingred, comparing scribbles with Verity as the girls tidied their hair for tea. "How anybody's expected to get down all Miss Strong tells us, I can't imagine! It's impossible."

"I don't try," admitted Fil. "At least I do try - I put a bit here and there, but I write so slowly, I'm only half-way through before she's bounced on to something else, and I've missed the beginning of it. I have to stop, too, sometimes, to think how to spell the words."

The others laughed, for Fil's spelling was proverbial in the form, and was often of a purely phonetic character. Miss Strong had periodical crusades to improve it, but generally gave them up as a bad job, and recommended constant use of a dictionary instead.

"Though you can't go about the world with a dictionary perpetually under your arm," she had remarked on the last occasion. "If you have to write a letter in a hurry, and you begin 'Dear Maddam' and end 'Yours trueley' - well! Please don't let anybody know you've been educated here, that's all, or it will be a poor advertisement for the College!"

Ingred was not at all delighted to be still in Miss Strong's form. She only moderately liked this mistress. Undoubtedly Miss Strong was a clever teacher, but sarcasm was one of her favorite weapons of discipline. Some of the girls did not mind it, indeed thought it rather amusing, even when directed against themselves, and enjoyed it hugely when someone else was the victim of the sally. Ingred, however, proud and sensitive, writhed under the attacks of Miss Strong's sharp tongue, and would often have preferred a punishment to a witticism. As a matter of fact, the mistress rarely gave punishments, and was proud of her ability to control her form without resorting to them. She was short in stature, but made up in spirit for her lack of inches, and would fix her dark eyes on offenders against discipline with the personal magnetism of a circus trainer or a leopard-tamer. Schoolgirls are irreverent beings, and though to her face her pupils showed her all respect, behind her back they spoke of her familiarly as "The Bantam," in allusion to her small size but plucky disposition, or sometimes, in reference to her sarcastic powers, as "The Sark," which by general custom became "The Snark." On the whole Miss Strong's pithy, racy, humorous style of teaching made her a far greater favorite than mistresses of duller caliber. She had a remarkable faculty for getting work out of the most unwilling brains. Her form always made excellent progress, and she had a reputation for obtaining record successes in examinations. To judge from the first few days of term, she meant to keep up her standard of efficiency. Miss Burd had mapped out a heavy time-table for VA., and it was Miss Strong's business to see that the girls got through it. Of course they grumbled. After the long weeks of the summer holidays it was doubly difficult to apply their minds to lessons, and set to work in the evenings to perform the enormous amount of preparation demanded from them. To some the task was wellnigh impossible, and poor Fil would send in very imperfect exercises, but others, Ingred and Verity among the number, had ambitions, and boosted up the record of the form.

It was after a most strenuous few days that Ingred came to the close of the first week of the new term, and, taking her books and hand-bag, started off to spend the week-end at home. She left the College with a feeling of intense relief. She had dreaded the return there, and the confession of her altered circumstances. It had not proved quite so disagreeable an ordeal as she had anticipated, for, after the first expressions of surprise, nobody had referred again to Rotherwood; yet Ingred, on the look-out for slights, imagined that she was not treated with as much consideration as formerly. Avis Marlowe and Jess Howard had hardly spoken to her, and, though the omission was probably owing to sheer lack of time or opportunity, she chose to set it down to a desire to show her the cold shoulder.

"Now I have no parties to offer them, they don't care about me!" she thought bitterly. "They'll hunt about till they find somebody else who's likely to act entertainer."

Fortunately, as Ingred stepped out of the College on that first Friday afternoon, the fresh breeze and the bright September sunshine blew away the cobwebs, and sent her almost dancing down the street. She had a naturally buoyant disposition, and her uppermost thought was: "I'm going home! I'm going home! Hurrah!"

The journey was really quite a little business. She had to take a tram to the Waterstoke terminus, then change on to a light electric railway that ran along the roadside for seven miles to Wynch-on-the-Wold. Grovebury, an old town that dated back to mediaeval times, lay in a deep hollow among a rampart of hills, so that, in whatever direction you left it, you were obliged to climb. The scenery was very beautiful, for trees edged the river, and clothed the slopes till they gave way to the gorse and heather of the wild moorlands. Wynch-on-the-Wold was a hamlet which, since the opening of the electric railway, was just beginning to turn into a suburb of Grovebury. Close to the terminus neat villas had sprung up like mushrooms; there were a few shops and a branch post office, and a brass plate to the effect that Dr. Whittaker had consulting hours twice a week. Tradesmen's carts drove out constantly, and the electric railway did quite a little business in the conveyance of parcels.

Wynchcote, the house where the Saxons had retired to try their scheme of retrenchment, lay at some little distance beyond the terminus, and might be considered the outpost of the new suburb. It was a small, picturesque modern bungalow; Mr. Saxon had built it as an architectural experiment, intending it for a sort of model country cottage. The tenants who had occupied it during the period of the war had just returned to Scotland, so, as it was vacant, it had seemed a convenient place in which to settle. It was near enough to Grovebury to allow him to attend his office, and far enough away to cut them adrift from old associations. After four and a half years of war work, Mrs. Saxon wanted a complete rest from committees, creches, canteens, and recreation huts, and would be glad to urge the excuse of distance to those who appealed for her help. Perhaps also she felt that in their straitened circumstances it was wiser to live where they could not enter into social competition with their former acquaintances.

"I just want to be quiet, to attend to my family, and to enjoy the moors and our garden," she declared. "I believe I'm going to be very happy at Wynchcote."

Though it was small, the bungalow was admirably planned, and had many advantages. The view from its French window was one of the finest in the district, and it faced a magnificent gorge, wild, rocky, and thickly wooded, at the bottom of which wound the silver river that ran through Grovebury. Civilization, in the shape of fields and hedges, stretched out fingers as far as Wynchcote, and there stopped abruptly. Past the bungalow lay the open wold with miles of heather, gorse, and bracken, and a road edged with low, grassy fern-covered banks instead of walls. The air blew freshly up here, and was far more bracing and healthy than down in the hollow of Grovebury. The residents of the new suburb affected seaside fashions, and went their moorland walks without hats or gloves.

Ingred was joined in the tram-car by Hereward, who attended the King George's School, and made the journey daily.

"Getting quite used to it now!" he assured his sister airily. "I had a terrific run yesterday for the train, but I caught it! There's another fellow in our form living up here, so we generally go together - Scampton, that chap in the cricket cap standing by the door. He's A1. He won't come near now, though, because he says he's terrified of girls. He's going to give me a rabbit, and I shall make a hutch for it out of one of those packing-cases. See, I've bought a piece of wire-netting for the door. There's heaps of room at the bottom of the garden. I believe I'll ask him to bring it over after tea."

"But the hutch isn't ready," objected Ingred.

"Oh, that won't matter! I can keep it in a packing-case for a day or two."

When Ingred and Hereward reached home they found that tea had been set out on the patch of grass under the apple trees, and Mother and Quenrede were sitting sewing and waiting for them. It was one of those beautiful September days when the air seems almost as warm as in August, and with the clock still at summer time, the sun had not climbed very far down the valley. The garden, where Mother and Quenrede had been working busily all the afternoon, was gay with nasturtiums and asters, and overhead hung a crop of the rosiest apples ever seen. Minx, the Persian cat, wandered round, waving a stately tail and mewing plaintively for her saucer of milk. Derry, the fox terrier, barked an enthusiastic greeting.

"Come along, you poor starving wanderers!" said Mrs. Saxon. "The kettle's boiling, and we'll make the tea in half a moment. Isn't it glorious here? Queenie and I have been digging up potatoes, and we quite enjoyed it. We felt exactly as if we were 'on the land.' How is your cold, Hereward? Ingred, you look tired, child! Sit down and rest while Queenie fetches the teapot."

Ingred sank into a garden-chair with much satisfaction. Wynchcote might not be Rotherwood, but it looked an uncommonly pretty little place in the September sunshine. To live there would be like a perpetual picnic. Mother and Queenie looked so complacently smiling that it seemed impossible to grouse, especially with newly-baked scones and rock-cakes on the tea-table.

The men kind of the family had not yet returned home. Mr. Saxon and Egbert rarely left their office before six, and

Athelstane had that day gone over to Birkshaw on the motor-bicycle, to arrange about the medical course which he was to take at the University. There was plenty of news, however, to be exchanged. Ingred had to give a full account of her experiences at school and hostel, and to hear in return the various achievements in the shape of home-carpentry, mending, making, and altering which are always an essential part of settling into a new establishment.

"I hardly feel I've been round the estate properly yet," she said, when tea was over, and she sat leaning back lazily in her deck-chair, with Minx purring upon her knee.

"Then come and lend me a hand with my rabbit-hutch," suggested Hereward. "Put down that wretched pampered beast of a cat, for goodness sake! If it gets at my new rabbit, I'll finish it! Yes, I will! I'll hang it or drown it! Get along, you brute!"

Hereward's blood-thirsty remarks were ignored by Minx, who, finding herself dropped from Ingred's lap, took a flying run up his back, and settled herself on his shoulder, rubbing her head into his neck. He scratched her under the chin, swung her gently down, and shook a reproving finger at her.

"Don't try to come round me with your blarneyings, you siren!" he declared. "Who was it ate my goldfinch? Yes, you may well look guilty! Don't blink your eyes at me like that! I haven't forgiven you yet, and I don't think I ever shall. Ingred, old sport, are you coming to help me, or are you not? I want some one to hold the wire."

"All right, Uncle Podger, I'll come and 'podge' for you," laughed Ingred. "Don't hammer my fingers, that's all I bargain for. Wait a moment till I get my overall. Your joinering performances are apt to be somewhat grubby and messy."

There was quite a good garden at the back of the bungalow, with rows of vegetables and gooseberry bushes and fruit-trees.

Angela Brazil

At the end was a wooden shed where the motor-bicycle was kept, and a small wired enclosure originally made for hens.

"It's exactly the place for rabbits, when I get a hutch for them," explained Hereward, putting down his box of tools, and turning over the packing-case with a professional eye. "Now a wooden frame covered with wire, and a pair of hinges will just do the job. I can saw these pieces to fit. Hold the wood steady, that's a mascot!"

The two were kneeling on the ground by the side of the packing-case, much absorbed in the process of exact measure-ments, when suddenly there was a rustling and a scrambling noise, and on the wall close to them appeared a collie dog, growling, snarling, and showing its teeth. Ingred sprang to her feet in alarm. Wynchcote was so retired that they had scarcely realized that its garden adjoined the garden of another house. The collie must have jumped up on to the dividing wall, and, being an ill-tempered beast, did not use proper discrimination between neighbors and tramps.

"Shoo! Get away!" urged Ingred, with rather shaking knees.

"Be off, you ill-mannered brute!" shouted Hereward.

The dog, however, appeared to think the wall was his own special property, and that it was his business to drive them away from their own garden. It continued to bark and snarl. Now, as Hereward wished to fix the rabbit-hutch in exactly the spot over which the creature had mounted guard, he was naturally much annoyed, and sought for some ready means of dislodging it from its point of vantage. He did not relish the prospect of being bitten, so did not want to engage it at close quarters, and no pole or other weapon lay handy.

Looking hastily round, his eye fell upon the garden-syringe with which Athelstane sometimes cleaned the motor-bicycle. It had been left, with a bucket of water, outside the shed. He drew out the piston, filled the syringe, then discharged its contents straight at the dog. But at that most unlucky moment a quick change took place on the wall; the collie retired in favor of his master, and the stream of water charged full into the astonished countenance of a precise and elderly gentleman from next door. For a few moments there was a ghastly silence, while he wiped his face and recovered his dignity. Then he demanded in withering tones:

"May I ask what is the meaning of this?"

Ingred and Hereward, overwhelmed with confusion, stuttered out apologies and explanations. The old gentleman listened with his busy gray eyebrows knitted and his mouth pursed into a thin line.

"I shall immediately take steps to ensure that my dog has no further opportunities of annoying you," he remarked stiffly, and took his departure.

"Who is he?" whispered Ingred, as the footsteps on the other side of the wall shuffled away.

"His name's Mr. Hardcastle. He's retired, and lives there with a housekeeper. Great Scot! I've put my foot in it, haven't I? Who'd have thought he was just going to pop his head up? Dad was going to ask him to lend us his garden-roller, but it's no use now. I expect I've made an enemy of him for life!"

"I hope he means to keep that savage dog fastened up," said Ingred. "It's a horrid idea to think that it may, any time, pounce over the wall at us. It's like having a wolf loose in the garden."

As a matter of fact, Mr. Hardcastle kept his word in a way that the Saxons least anticipated. Instead of chaining the dog, he had a tall wooden paling erected along the top of the wall, making an effectual barrier between the two gardens. It was not a beautiful object, and it cut off the sunshine from a whole long flower-bed; so, though it insured privacy, it might be regarded as a doubtful benefit for the bungalow.

"It makes one feel so suburban," mourned Quenrede.

"We shan't be visible, at any rate, when we're digging potatoes," laughed Mrs. Saxon, "and that's a great point to me, for I'm past the age that looks fascinating in an overall. If we've Suburbia on one side of us, we've the open moor on the other, which is something to be thankful for."

"Yes, until it's sold in building plots," sighed Quenrede, who was in a fit of blues, and unwilling to count up her blessings.

# CHAPTER IV

## INTRUDER BESS

Ingred, after a blissful week-end, returned to Grovebury by the early train on Monday morning, and, wrenching her mind with difficulty from the interests of Wynch-on-the-Wold, focused it on school affairs instead. There was certainly need of mental concentration if she meant to make headway in the College. The standard of work required from VA. was very stiff, and taxed the powers of even the brightest girls to the uttermost.

"Miss Strong reminds me of Rehoboam!" wailed Fil, fresh from the study of the Second Book of Chronicles. "Her little finger's thicker than her whole body used to be, and, instead of whips, she chastises us with scorpions. I want to go and bow the knee to Baal."

"Rather mixed up in your Scripture, child, but we understand your meaning," laughed Verity. "The Bantam's certainly piling it on nowadays in the way of prep."

"Shows an absolutely brutal lack of consideration," agreed Nora.

"So do all the mistresses," groaned Ingred. "Each of them seems to think we've nothing to do but her own particular subject. Dr. Linton actually asked me if I could practise two hours a day. Why, he might as well have suggested four! I can

Angela Brazil

only get the piano for an hour, even if I wanted it longer. It's a frightful business at the hostel to cram in all our practicing, isn't it? I nearly had a free fight with Janie Potter yesterday. She commandeered the piano, and though I showed her the music time-table, with my name down for '5 to 6' she wouldn't budge. I had to tilt her off the stool in the end. It was like a game of musical chairs. She wouldn't look at me to-day, she's so cross about it. Not that *I* care in the least!"

Music was a favorite subject with Ingred, and one in which she excelled. She would willingly have given more time to it, had the school curriculum allowed. She was a good reader, and had a sympathetic, if rather spidery touch. This term she had begun lessons with Dr. Linton, who was considered the best master in Grovebury. He was organist at the Abbey Church, and was not only a Doctor of Music, but a composer as well. His anthems and cantatas were widely known, he conducted the local choral society and trained the operatic society for the annual performance. His time was generally very full, so he did not profess to teach juniors; it was only after celebrating her fifteenth birthday that Ingred had been eligible as one of his pupils. He had the reputation of being peppery tempered, therefore she walked into the room to take her first lesson with her heart performing a sort of jazz dance under her jersey. Dr. Linton, like many musicians, was of an artistic and excitable temperament, and highly eccentric. Instead of sitting by the side of his new pupil, he paced the room, pursing his lips in and out, and drawing his fingers through his long lank dark hair.

"Have you brought a piece with you," he inquired. "Then play to me. Oh, never mind if you make mistakes! That's not the point. I want to know how you can talk on the piano. What have you got in that folio? Beethoven? Rachmaninoff? M'Dowell? We'll try the Beethoven. Now don't be nervous. Just fire away as if you were practising at home!"

It was all very well, Ingred thought, for Dr. Linton to tell her not to be nervous, but it was a considerable ordeal to have to perform a test piece before so keen a critic. In spite of her most valiant efforts her hands trembled, and wrong chords crept in. She kept bravely at it, however, and managed to reach the end of the first movement, where she called a halt.

"It's not talking - it's only stuttering and stammering on the piano," she apologized.

Dr. Linton laughed. Her remark had evidently pleased him. He always liked a pupil who fell in with his humor.

"You've the elements of speech in you, though you're still in the prattling-baby stage," he conceded. "It's something, at any rate, to find there's material to work upon. Some people wouldn't make musicians if they practised for a hundred years. We've got to alter your touch - your technique's entirely wrong - but if you're content to concentrate on that, we'll soon show some progress. You'll have to stick to simple studies this term: no blazing away into M'Dowell and Rachmaninoff yet awhile."

"I'll do anything you tell me," agreed Ingred humbly.

Dr. Linton's manner might be brusque, but he seemed prepared to take an interest in her work. He was known to give special pains to those whose artistic caliber appealed to him. In his opinion pupils fell under two headings: those who had music in them, and those who had not. The latter, though he might drill them in technique, would never make really satisfactory pianists; the former, by dint of scolding or cajoling, according to his mood at the moment, might derive real benefit from his tuition, and become a credit to him. It was a by-word in the school that his favorites had the stormiest lessons.

"I'm thankful I'm not a pet pupil," declared Fil, whose playing was hardly of a classical order. "I should have forty fits if he stalked about the room, and tore his hair, and shouted like he does with Janie. He scared me quite enough sitting by my side

Angela Brazil

and saying: 'Shall we take this again now?' with a sort of grim politeness, as if he were making an effort to restrain his temper. I know I'm not what he calls musical, but I can't help it. I'd rather hear comic opera any day than his wretched cantatas, and when I'm not practising I shall play what I like. There!"

And Fil, who was sitting at the piano, twirled round on the stool and strummed "Beautiful K - K - Katie" with a lack of technique that probably would have brought her teacher's temper up to bubbling-over point had he been there to listen to her.

It was exactly ten days after the term had begun that Bess Haselford came to the College. She walked into the Upper Fifth Form room one Monday morning, looking very shy and lost and strange, and stood forlornly, not knowing where to sit, till somebody took pity on her, and pointed to a vacant desk. It happened to be on a line with Ingred's, and the latter watched her settle herself. She looked her over with the critical air that is generally bestowed on new girls, and decided that she was particularly pretty. Bess was the image of one of the Sir Joshua Reynolds' child angels in the National Gallery. The likeness was so great that her mother had always cut and curled her golden-brown hair in exact copy of the picture. She was a slim, rosy, bright-eyed, smiling specimen of girlhood, and, though on this first morning she was manifestly afflicted with shyness, she had the appearance of one whose acquaintance might be worth making. Ingred decided to cultivate it at the earliest opportunity, and spoke to the new arrival at lunch-time. Bess replied readily to the usual questions.

"We've only come lately to Grovebury. We used to live at Birkshaw. Yes, I'm fairly keen on hockey, though I like tennis better. Have you asphalt courts here, and do you play in the winter? I adore dancing, but I hate gym. I'm learning the violin, and I'm to start oil-painting this term."

She seemed such a pleasant, winsome kind of girl that Ingred, who was apt to take sudden fancies, constituted herself her cicerone, and showed her round the school. By the time they had made the entire tour of the buildings, Ingred began to wonder whether, without offense, it would be possible to leave her desk, next to Verity, and sit beside Bess. There was a great charm of voice and manner about the new-comer, and Ingred's musical ear was sensitive to gentle voices. She discussed Bess with the others next morning before school.

"Yes, she's pretty, and that blue dress is simply adorable," conceded Nora. "I'm going to have an embroidered one myself next time."

"Her hair is so sweet," commented Francie.

"I call her ripping!" said Ingred with enthusiasm.

"Well, you ought to take an interest in her, Ingred, considering that she lives at Rotherwood," put in Beatrice.

"At Rotherwood!"

"Yes, didn't you know *that*?"

Ingred, under pretence of distributing exercise-books, turned hastily away. Her heart was in a sudden turmoil. This was indeed a bolt from the blue. She, of course, knew that Rotherwood was let, but she had not heard the name of the tenants, and, as the subject was a sore one, had forborne to ask any questions at home. It was surely the irony of fate that the house should be taken by people who had a daughter of her own age, and that this daughter should come to the College, and actually be placed in the same form as herself. She seemed a rival ready-made. Biased by jealous prejudice, Ingred's hastily-formed judgment reversed itself.

"I'm thankful I didn't move away from Verity to sit next to her," she thought. "I expect she'll be ever so conceited and give herself airs, and the other girls will truckle to her no end. I know them! I wish to goodness she hadn't come to the

College. Why didn't they send her away to a boarding school? I'm not going to make a fuss over her, so she needn't think it."

Poor Bess, quite unaware of being any cause of offence, and grateful for the kindness shown her the day before, greeted Ingred in most friendly fashion, and looked amazement itself at the cool reception of her advances. She stared for a moment as if hardly believing the evidence of her eyes and ears, then turned away with a hurt look on her pretty, sensitive face.

Ingred shut her desk with a slam. She was feeling very uncomfortable. She had liked Bess with a kind of love-at-first-sight, and if the latter had come to live at any other house in the town than Rotherwood, would have been prepared to go on liking her. Generosity whispered that her conduct was unjust, but at this particular stage of Ingred's evolution she did not always listen to those inner voices that act as our highest guides. Like most of us, she had a mixed character, capable of many good things but with certain failings. Rotherwood was what the girls called "the bee in her bonnet," and the knowledge that Bess was in possession of the beautiful home she had lost was sufficient to check the incipient friendship.

It was otherwise with the rest of the form. They frankly welcomed the new-comer, and if they did not, as Ingred had bitterly prognosticated, exactly "truckle" to her, they certainly began to treat her as a favorite. She was asked at once to join the Photographic Society and the Drawing Club, and her very superior camera, beautiful color-box, and other up-to-date equipments were immensely admired. Ingred, on the outside of the enthusiastic circle, preserved a stony silence. Her own camera was three years old, and she did not possess materials for oil-painting. She thought it quite unnecessary for Verity to want to look at Bess's paraphernalia. Verity, who was a kind-hearted little soul, perhaps divined the cause of her chum's glumness, for she came presently and took Ingred's arm.

"I've something to tell you, Ingred," she whispered. "We are to have the election on Friday afternoon, and everybody's saying you'll be chosen warden for the form."

"Don't suppose I've the remotest chance!" grunted Ingred gloomily.

"Nonsense! Don't be a blue-bottle! Cheery-ho! In my opinion you'll just have an easy walk over."

With the removal into the new building, Miss Burd had instituted many innovations and changes. Among the most important of these was the College Council, which really served as a sort of House of Parliament for the school. Each form among the seniors and intermediates was to elect a representative called a warden, and these, with such permanent officers as the prefects and the games captain, were to meet once a fortnight to discuss questions of self-government. It was a new experiment, and the head mistress hoped it would give the girls some idea of responsibility, and train them to understand civic duties later on. The girls themselves voted it a "ripping" idea. They took it up most enthusiastically. It would be fun to have elections, and it seemed desirable that there should be a warden to look after the interests of each separate form.

"When I was in the Fourth we never got a chance for the tennis courts, and it was utterly hopeless to appeal to the prefects," said Ingred. "I always used to feel there ought to be some way of making one's voice heard."

"Well, if you're elected, you'll have a chance to make your maiden speech!" laughed Verity. "By the bye, will there be a 'Strangers' Gallery, so that we can come and listen to you? I'd be sorry to miss the fun!"

Friday afternoon had been fixed for the election, and a bright idea originated in VA., circulated through the school, and finally crystallized in the Sixth. It was nothing less than that each form should make a special fete of the affair. Lispeth Scott, the head girl, went boldly to Miss Burd, and asked permission for those who liked to bring thermos flasks, cups, and bags of buns and cakes, and hold parties in the various class-rooms.

"It would make so much more of the whole thing," she urged. "If we simply stop for ten minutes after school and vote, I'm afraid it may fall rather flat. But if every form has its festival to elect its own warden, it will make the council seem a much more important business. We'd like to be allowed to stay till about half-past five, if we may, so that there would be time to have some fun over it. We'd promise not to make a mess with our picnicking."

Miss Burd, looking rather astonished, nevertheless consented. She was a wise woman, and believed in permitting a certain amount of liberty, within limits.

"You may try it this once," she conceded. "But it's on the distinct understanding that you're all on your good behavior. I shall hold you prefects responsible for controlling the school. If you hear a great noise, you must go into their form-rooms and stop them. I can't allow the College to be turned into a bear-garden."

"We won't! I'll put them all on their honor to behave, and I'll leave the door of our form-room open so that I can hear what's going on. Thank you so much, Miss Burd!"

And Lispeth departed, fearful lest any other qualifications should be added to temper the joy of the proceedings.

Six girls, waiting outside the door to hear the result of the negotiations, waved signals of success to others farther down the corridor, and, in an almost incredibly short space of time, the happy news had spread to the remotest corners of the school.

"But how are we hostelites going to manage our share?" asked Ingred anxiously.

"Don't you worry about that," Jess and Francie assured her. "Ten girls in our form have promised to bring thermos flasks, and if we pool to tea there'll be heaps to go round, and the same with buns and cakes. We'll each bring a little extra to make enough. The hostel will very likely lend you each a cup if you ask for it. That's all you'll need!"

"Right-o! We'll cast ourselves on the charity of the form!" agreed Ingred.

# CHAPTER V

## THE FIFTH-FORM FETE

By a general indulgence issued from head-quarters, the dismissal bell rang at 3:45 the next Friday afternoon, instead of, as usual, at four o'clock. The mistresses entered up the marks, put away their books, said "Good afternoon, girls!" and made their exit, leaving the building for once in the sole possession of the pupils. Miss Strong, indeed, who disapproved of the whole business, took the precaution of locking her desk before her departure, a proceeding which provoked indignant sniffs from the witnesses; but, sublimely indifferent to public opinion, she put the key in her pocket, and stalked from the room. The girls gave her a few moments' grace to get out of earshot, then broke into a babble of conversation.

"Which are we having first, the election or the tea?"

"Oh, the tea!"

"No, no! Business first and pleasure afterwards."

"I can't vote till I've had some tea."

"It's too early!"

"No, it isn't! We're most of us ready for it."

"Look here!" suggested Ingred. "Let's settle it this way. Have tea first, then the election, and then some fun afterwards. Don't you think that would sandwich things best?"

"True, O Queen! I don't mind what happens afterwards, so long as I get a bun quick!"

"Let's fetch the prog," agreed Linda Slater, leading the way towards the cloak-room where the baskets had been stored.

The giggling procession met emissaries from other forms, bent on a like errand, and exchanged a brisk banter as they passed on the stairs.

"We've got jam tartlets!"

"Not as nice as our cheese cakes!"

"Nellie's brought a whole pound of macaroons!"

"Oh! will you swap with us for rock buns?"

"I should just think not!"

"Dolly Arden has five oranges!"

"Well, we've got bananas!"

After successfully fetching the provisions, having routed a marauding band of juniors who were poking inquisitive fingers into the baskets, the members of VA. returned to the form-room, closed the door, and gave themselves up to festivity. The four girls from the hostel need have had no fear of scarcity, for the others had brought ample to compensate for their deficiency. By general consent all the cakes were pooled, set out on hard-backed exercise books in lieu of plates, and handed round the company. Bess, whose basket contained two thermos flasks, a dozen cheese cakes, and some meringues, was felt to have brought a valuable contribution. It seemed a new experience to be sitting at their desks, drinking tea and eating cakes, instead of doing translation or writing exercises.

"Pity the Snark didn't stop! She doesn't know what she's missing!" remarked Joanna Powers, as she took a meringue.

"Oh, Kafoozalum! We shouldn't have had much fun if the Snark had stayed! Don't bring her back, for goodness' sake, Jo!"

"I wasn't going to! Besides which, she's probably half-way down town at present, having tea in a cafe. She generally does on Fridays."

"She won't get a better tea than we're having!"

"I'll undertake she won't! This meringue is absolutely topping! I wonder if there's another left."

"No, they're gone, every one of them!"

"Hard luck!"

Though the hour might be early, the girls' appetites were quite equal to the task of finishing the various delicacies in the way of sweet stuff which they had brought with them. Cakes disappeared like snow in summer, and chocolate boxes, passed round impartially, soon returned empty to their owners. When everything seemed almost finished, Bess produced another hamper, which she had carried up from the cloak-room, and stowed away under her desk. She handed it rather shyly to Beatrice, who happened to be her nearest neighbor.

"Mother sent these, and wants you all to share them," she remarked.

Beatrice, Francie, and Linda opened the hamper all three together, then with a delighted "O-Oh!" of satisfaction drew out six beautiful bunches of purple grapes. Ingred, finishing her cup of tea, choked and coughed. She knew those grapes well. They grew in the vinery at Rotherwood, and had been the pride of her father and of the head-gardener. She had not tasted one of them for five years, for during the war they had always been given to the patients in the Red Cross Hospital, but she could not forget their delicious flavor. Why had her father let the vinery with the house? The grapes ought to be hers to give away - not this girl's. Nobody else in the room cared in the least where the fruit came from, so long as it was there. Appreciative eyes looked on in glad anticipation while Beatrice and Francie divided the bunches with as much mathematical accuracy as they could muster at the moment. A portion was laid upon each desk, and the girls fell to.

"Delicious!"

"Never tasted better in my life!"

"Absolutely topping!"

"Makes one want to go and live in a vineyard!"

"They're exactly ripe!"

"Ingred, you're not eating yours!"

"I don't want them, thanks," said Ingred hurriedly. "I don't indeed. I've had enough. Pass them on to somebody else, please!"

"Well, if you really don't want them, they won't go a-begging, I dare say!"

Ingred felt as if the grapes would choke her. She could not touch one of them. She hated Bess for having brought them to school, quite irrespective of the fact that she would have done exactly the same in her place, had she been fortunate enough to have the opportunity. Bess, looking shy, and anxious to evade the thanks that poured in upon her, bundled the hamper away under the desk again, and made a palpable effort to change the subject.

"What about this election?" she asked. "Time's getting on. It's after half-past four."

"Good night! Have we been all that time feeding? Here, girls, if you've *quite* finished, let's get to business," said Avis, rapping on her desk as a signal for silence, and constituting herself spokeswoman for the occasion. "You know what we've met here for - to choose a warden to represent us on the School Council. Well, I feel we couldn't do better than send up Ingred Saxon. She'd look after our interests all right, if anybody would. I beg to propose Ingred Saxon."

"And I beg to second that!" called Nora.

"Hands up, those in favor!"

Such a forest of arms immediately waved in the air that (though in strict order) it seemed hardly necessary for Avis to call out:

"Those against!"

No opposition hands appeared, so without further discussion the election was carried.

"Congrats, Ingred!" said Nora, patting the heroine on the back.

"I told you it would be a walk over, old sport!" whispered Verity.

"We'd talked it over beforehand, you see, and everybody had agreed to choose you, so it was really only a matter of form," explained Francie.

"The Sixth are having a ballot," put in Jess.

"And VB. are going to fight like Kilkenny cats over Magsie and Barbara."

"There'll be some hullabaloo in several of the forms, I expect."

"Thanks awfully for electing me," replied Ingred. "I suppose I ought to make a speech, but I really don't know what to say!"

"You've got to say it all the same!" laughed Verity. "Members of Parliament always make speeches to their constituents. Here, take the Snark's desk as your thingumgig - rostrum, or whatever it's called, and begin your jaw-wag!"

"Friends, Romans, Countrymen, lend me your ears!" squeaked Kitty Saunders.

Pushed forward by a dozen hands, Ingred found herself occupying the mistress's place, and, facing her audience, made a valiant attempt at oratory. With cheeks aglow, and dark eyes shining like stars, she looked an attractive little figure, and a bright and suitable leader for the form.

"I can't really think why you should have chosen me," she began ("don't be too modest!" yelled a voice from the back), "but as you *have* made me your warden, I'll take care that all our grievances are very well aired at the School Council." ("You'll have your work cut out!" interrupted Francie.) "Of course I know it won't all be plain sailing, and that the Sixth need a great deal of sticking up to over many matters." ("That's so!" came from the front desk.) "But perhaps they'll be prepared to talk things over now, and make some concessions." ("Time they did!") "At any rate, I shall be able to tell them what you all think" ("Flattering for them!"), "and to make things as smooth as possible for VA. Now, as I'm warden, may I propose that we have some fun before we go? Shall we have music, or games? Hands up for an Emergency Concert!"

"A very neat way of getting out of further speechifying!" said

Angela Brazil

Verity, as by general consent the concert carried the day; "but you shall open it yourself, Madam Warden, so I warn you! You're not going to be let off, don't you think it! Silence! Ladies and gentlemen, the first item on the program will be a piano solo by Miss Ingred Saxon, the celebrated musical star, brought over at enormous expense, on purpose for this occasion."

"You blighter!" murmured Ingred, as the prospective audience shouted "Hear! Hear!"

"Not a bit of it!" purred Verity. "I guess we'll take sparks out of the Sixth and everybody else."

VA. that afternoon was certainly in a position to boast itself. It was the only form in possession of a piano: for by the sheerest accident it had one. The instrument was only a temporary visitor, placed there for convenience while some repairs were being done to a leaking gas-pipe in one of the music rooms. It's an ill wind, however, that blows nobody good, and it gave VA. an opportunity that was denied even to the Sixth. Ingred was at once escorted to the piano, and officious hands piled exercise books on a chair to make her seat high enough.

"I can't remember anything! I can't indeed!" she protested vigorously.

"Now don't twitter nonsense!" said Nora. "I've heard you play dozens - yes, *dozens*! - of things without music at the hostel, so you've just got to try!"

"I shall break down, I know I shall!"

"Then you can begin again at the beginning. Fire away, and don't be affected!" commanded Nora.

It is one thing to play a piece from memory when you have the room to yourself, and quite another to play it with half a dozen girls hanging over the piano, and the rest of the audience sitting on their desks. Ingred wisely did not venture on anything too classical, but tried a bright "Spanish Ballade," and managed to get successfully to the end of it without any breakdown. In the midst of the clapping that followed came a loud rap-tap-tap at the door, which immediately opened to admit - much to the astonishment of the Fifth - two of the prefects, and a consignment of Sixth form girls.

"Whatever have we been and gone and done now?" murmured Verity.

"Is music taboo?" asked Ingred guiltily, slipping away from the piano.

The errand of the prefects, however, was evidently one of conciliation, and not of reproof. They were smiling, and looking amiability itself.

"We thought, as you've got a piano in your room," began Lilias Ashby, "that we might as well come and join you, if you don't mind. Janie's got a book of songs with her."

"Oh, by all means, of course!" replied VA. politely and unanimously. "We're just having a sort of concert, you know."

"Sure you don't mind?"

"Not a bit of it!"

"Right-o! Run and tell Janie then, Susie, and ask her to bring the others."

An invasion from the Sixth was indeed an unwonted honor, which probably nothing short of a piano would have accomplished. The hostesses, somewhat overwhelmed, seated the distinguished guests to the best of their ability in the rather limited accommodation, and hospitably passed round their few remaining pieces of chocolate.

"We'll leave the door open, please," said Lispeth, "because I promised Miss Burd not to let those intermediates get too outrageous, and I have to listen out for them."

Janie Potter, with her book of songs, was pushed forward, and began to entertain the company with popular selections of the day, to which they chanted the choruses. She had a good clear voice, and the audience joined with enthusiasm in the various ditties.

The clapping which followed was continued down the landing, and, through the open door, peered the interested faces of most of the members of VB. who had come to share the fun.

"May we butt in?" they asked hopefully.

"Not a square inch of room for you," answered Lispeth, "but you may squat in the corridor outside if you like. Anybody who performs can join the show, but that's all. I'll tell you when it's your turn. It's VA. next. Now then," (turning to the hostesses), "who else can do anything? Francie Hall, come along at once!"

"I can't! I can't!" objected Francie. "So it's no use asking me; it isn't indeed! I'll tell you what - Bess Haselford plays the violin, and, what's more, she's got it with her, for I saw her put it away in the dressing-room."

"O-O-Oh! It was my lesson with Signor Chianti this afternoon, that's why I had to bring it!" said Bess, turning red.

"Go and fetch it, Francie!" ordered Lispeth. "You know where it is."

Francie returned in a short time, and handed the neat leather case to its owner. Bess, looking flustered and nervous, drew out the violin, and began to tune it.

"I've brought your music too!" said Francie, triumphantly

opening a folio, "so you've no excuse for saying you can't remember anything. Who'll play your accompaniment? Here, Ingred!"

"Oh! somebody else would do it far better," protested Ingred. "Janie -"

"I'm no reader."

"Lilas?"

"Couldn't to save my life!"

"Go ahead, Ingred, and don't waste time!" said Lispeth firmly.

Ingred sat down to the piano without a smile. Her schoolmates took her unwillingness for modesty, but in her heart of hearts her main thought was: "Why should *I* help this new girl to show off?" She would have played accompaniments gladly for anybody else, but she considered that Bess had already received quite enough attention in one afternoon. For her own credit, however, she must do her best, so she concentrated her energies on the prelude. When the first strains of the violin joined in, her musical ear recognized immediately that Bess's playing was of a very high quality. The tone was pure, the notes were perfectly in tune, and there was a ringing sweetness, a crisp power of expression, and a haunting pathos in the rendering of the melody that showed the performer to be capable of interpreting the composer's meaning. In spite of her disinclination, Ingred warmed to the accompaniment. When the violin seemed to be bringing out laughter and tears, the piano must do its part, and not merely supply a succession of unimpassioned chords. Ingred was a good reader for a girl of fifteen, but she surpassed herself on this occasion, and seemed to accomplish the difficult passages almost by instinct. She played the final notes very softly as the last fairy strains of the melody thrilled slowly away.

There was a second of silence, then the girls, inside and outside the room, clapped their loudest.

"It was capital!" declared Lispeth encouragingly. "Bess, we shall want you again for school concerts. You and Ingred ought to practise together. Let me look at your violin. I wish *I* could play like that!"

"Thanks ever so much!" murmured Bess to Ingred, as the latter got up from the piano.

"Oh! it's all right!" replied Ingred airily, moving away in a hurry to the other side of the room. She did not want Bess to take up Lispeth's no doubt well meant but rather embarrassing suggestion that they should practise together, and was quite ready with an excuse if it should be proposed.

"It's the turn of the Sixth now," she jodelled.

"VB. haven't done anything yet; I'll call one of them in," said Lispeth, stepping out to the landing.

Once through the door, however, her ears were assailed by such an absolute din proceeding from the farther end of the corridor, that she dropped her character of impresario for the duties of head-girl, and calling two of her fellow prefects, went to investigate the cause of the disturbance. She returned in a short time, looking flushed and flurried.

"It's those wretched kids in IVB.," she proclaimed. "They were behaving disgracefully, pelting each other with the remains of their buns, and fencing with rulers. And they actually had the cheek to tell me they weren't making any more noise than we were with our singing and playing! I sent them home at once, and I think we'd all better go too. Those intermediates always overstep the line if they've an atom of a chance. I told them what I thought about them. It's been quite a ripping concert, and I'm sorry to break it up, but you understand, don't you?"

"Rather!" replied the others, as they began their exodus into the corridor.

# CHAPTER VI

## THE SCHOOL PARLIAMENT

During the excitement of the concert Ingred had hardly time to realize the greatness of the honor thrust upon her in being chosen as warden to represent her form. All it stood for struck her afterwards.

"My word! You'll have to sit up and behave yourself after this, Madame!" remarked Quenrede, when she mentioned the matter at home.

"Yes, of course they'll all look to you now as an example!" added Mother.

"Oh, I don't think they will!" declared Ingred, who had not considered her new office from that point of view. "I've just to speak up for the interests of the form, you know."

"There are obligations as well as interests," said Mother seriously. "Try to make VA. a useful factor in the school. That would be something worth doing, wouldn't it?"

In arranging for the School Parliament, Miss Burd had allowed wardens to be chosen by each form, from IIIB. upwards, but had decided that the smaller girls were too young to take part in public affairs. Every form that sent a representative constituted itself into a kind of club, and chose a special name. These were placed on the Council Register as follows:

VI. The True Blues.
VA. The Pioneers.
VB. The Amazons.
IVA. The Old Brigade.
IVB. The Mermaids.
IIIA. The Dragonflies.
IIIB. The Cuckoos.

"You can compare marks every fortnight," said Miss Burd, "and whichever gets the best average shall hold a cup that I intend to present. The marks of the whole form will count, so that slackers will be a distinct drawback to their own companies. Any girl who loses a mark hinders her form from gaining the cup, and of course vice versa, those who work will help."

The question of marks had been a much debated subject with Miss Burd. She had discussed it in detail at several educational conferences, and had come to the conclusion that, on the whole, the system was highly desirable.

"It's all very well to talk about the evils of emulation, and work for work's sake," she confided to Miss Strong, "but you can't get children to see things altogether in the same light as grown-ups. I own that, when I was a child myself, I made tremendous efforts so that I might be head of my form, and when the arrangements were changed at our school, and, instead of carefully-registered marks and places, we only had first, second, or third class, I slacked off considerably. I knew that a lesson not quite so perfectly learnt, or an exercise with one or two mistakes, would still find me in the First Class, so why should I make such enormous exertions? When every slip might mean the loss of my chance to be top, I was far more careful. Of course I know that Emulation, with a big E, is supposed to be all wrong, but really I think people make too much fuss about it. It was quite friendly rivalry when I was at school, and the girls with whom I competed were my dearest chums. I believe my new system here is going to unite both methods. Every girl will work for herself, but her marks will also count for her

Angela Brazil

form, and if she slacks, and so pulls down the standard, I hope her companions will give her as bad a time as they do to a 'butter-fingers' at cricket, and that's saying something!"

The idea of each form constituting a club appealed to the school. It was far more interesting to be "Amazons" or "Cuckoos" than merely VB. or IIIB., and as awards were to be according to averages, it was thrilling to feel that girls of twelve could wrest away the silver cup from the hands of the very prefects themselves.

"It makes it just like playing a game!" declared Ida Brooke.

"Yes, a sort of tug-of-war when everybody's got to pull, and mustn't let go!" added Cissie Barnes, "Do you remember playing 'Oranges and Lemons' once with the Sixth? We all held on to each others' waists like grim death, and Janie Potter gave way and broke their chain, so we won!"

"We'll beat them again, too! I'd like to see that cup on our mantelpiece!"

"The Pioneers," otherwise VA., were as anxious as any of the other forms to carry off laurels. Even Fil, much under protest, really made quite an effort to work.

"You ought to help me with my exercises, though, Ingred," she wheedled. "Remember, it's for the benefit of the form. If you let me make mistakes, well - it's the form that will suffer. You can't call it *my* fault, it's on your own head. You know as well as I do that I simply can't spell, and it takes me hours to hunt up words in the dictionary. I'm looking for 'phenomenon' now."

"You certainly won't find it in the F's," laughed Ingred. "What an infant in arms you are! Here, then, go ahead, and I'll act as dictionary. You've only written half a page yet. You'll be a week of Sundays at this rate."

"And I haven't touched my Latin or French!" sighed Fil dismally. "I wish I could go to a school where there isn't any homework, and that somebody would invent a typewriter that would just spell the words ready-made when you press a button."

"There's a fortune waiting for the man who does!" agreed Ingred. "'The Royal-Road-to-Learning Typewriter: spells of itself.' It would sell by the million, I should think."

Ingred washed her hands, plaited her hair, and put on her best brooch and her new bangle to attend the first meeting of the School Parliament. The function was held in the Sixth Form room, which she thought slightly unfair, for the prefects, being on their own ground, felt a distinct advantage, and acted as hostesses. There were four of them, so with the games captain they made a party of five from the Sixth, as opposed to six representatives of lower forms, a quite undue proportion in the opinion of the younger girls. Whatever successes the interme-diates might win later on, "The True Blues" had carried all before them so far, and had won the cup by an average at least a dozen marks in advance of "The Mermaids," who came second. The trophy stood on their mantelpiece, and they had brought an ornamental glazed tile on which to place it, as if they meant it to stay there.

On the whole they received the other wardens very graciously, and gave them opportunities to speak and air their views. Questions such as the due apportioning of the asphalt tennis-courts, basket-ball and hockey fixtures, and various school societies were discussed, and the general business of the term got under way.

"It helps things to be able to talk it over and know what you all think," said Lispeth. "We're making so many changes with coming into the new building, that it's almost like an entirely fresh start. Miss Burd wants us to get up a sort of Recons-truction Society in the school. She hasn't quite planned it out yet, but she told me a little about it, and I think it's ever so nice. As soon as it's quite fixed up, I'm going to call a general meeting, and explain it to everybody. I expect that will be next Wednesday. Will you give me power to do this on my own, or must I call a special committee on Monday to discuss it first, before I put it to the school?"

"It's my music lesson on Monday, I couldn't come," demurred Ingred.

"And I have to go to the dentist immediately after four," chimed in Alys Horner, the warden of "The Amazons."

"If Miss Burd has arranged it, I suppose it's all serene," said Mabel Hughes, of "The Old Brigade."

"You'll like it, I know. I'd explain now, only I haven't got any of the papers, and besides, it would take such a long time, and it's rather late, and I want to be getting home. Anyway, I hope we shall all take it up hot and strong. Be sure to keep Wednesday free, though I'm going to ask Miss Burd to let us have the meeting in school hours if possible, then we're absolutely sure of everybody."

"Right you are!" agreed the wardens, separating in a rather unparliamentary fashion to admire a vinaigrette, scented with heliotrope, which Althea took from her pocket and handed round for appreciative sniffs.

All the girls felt that Lispeth Scott was to be trusted. She was a worthy leader for the new order of things. She was a tall, stout, fair girl of almost eighteen, and rather grown-up for her age. She was the youngest member of a large family who had made enormous exertions during the war, and, with sisters who had nursed in Serbia, driven motor-ambulances in France, served in canteens, in Y. M. C. A. huts, and worked at munitions, she had excellent examples of what it is possible to do for one's country. She was a decided favorite in the College, being athletic as well as clever, and of a very jolly merry temperament with a vein of great earnestness. Though the girls sometimes called her "Jumbo," they meant the nickname in token of friendship, and submitted to her dictatorship far more readily than they would have done to that of any other member of the Sixth who had been put in her place. Miss Burd had great confidence in Lispeth, and consequently, when they had talked over the matter of the new society which she wished to be formed in the school, she decided to leave its institution entirely in the hands of her head girl.

"It will be far better for the mistresses not to be present at the meeting," she said. "I can trust you, Lispeth, to explain things, and the girls will like it much more if it seems to emanate from the new Council. Talk to them in your own way, and they'll understand you. I want the Society to be an absolutely voluntary one, or it's of no use. Don't let them think they must join merely to please *me*. I'd rather have a dozen who are in earnest over it than a hundred half-hearted members. Only those who feel enthusiastic need give in their names. I don't mind if it begins in quite a humble way. Indeed, I only expect a small membership at first."

"On the contrary, Miss Burd, I think it will catch on," replied Lispeth.

In consequence of this conversation, the head prefect pinned a paper on the notice-board, convening a general meeting of all girls over twelve years of age, to be held in the big hall on Wednesday afternoon at 3:30 sharp, the last lesson of the day having been remitted by orders from the Study. There was a universal feeling that something important was on foot, so those forms that were eligible trooped in a body to the hall, while the disappointed juniors tried to console themselves with the reflection that they would be able to go home half an hour earlier than their elders. After considerable shuffling about, places were taken. Unwilling to waste further time, Lispeth mounted the platform, and rang the bell for silence.

"Are we all here? Well, I can't wait for anybody else. Those who come in late will have to hear what they can, and you must tell them the rest afterwards. Oh, here they are! Quietly, please! There's plenty of room over there. Violet, will you shut the door? Now that we're all together, I want to have a talk with you. You know I'm what may be called 'Prime Minister' of our School Parliament, and, though your wardens will report all we say in council, I think it is well to have a public meeting sometimes. This term everything seems to have made a fresh start. We're in new buildings, and we have new rules, and our very Parliament is a new institution. You're all in new forms, and I'm the new Head Prefect. It's not only in school that everything's different, but in the outside world as well. This is our first term since peace was signed. I can remember our first term after War was declared. I was only in IIIA. then - quite a youngster! Hetty Hughes, who was the head girl, made a speech, and told us what we ought to do to try to help our country. I think some of us who were here have never forgotten that. We nearly hurrahed the roof off, and we formed a Knitting Club and a Soldiers' Parcel Society on the spot. You know for yourselves how we worked to keep those up. Well, to-day the Empire is at peace, but our country needs our help as much as ever, or even more. It's making a fresh start, and we want the new world to be a better place than the old. Hundreds of thousands of gallant young lives have been gladly given to establish this new world - in this school alone we know to our cost - and we owe it to our heroic dead not to let their sacrifice be in vain. We want a better and purer England to rise up and make a clean sweep of the bad things that disgraced her before. I expect you'll say: 'Oh, that's for politicians, and not for us schoolgirls!' but it isn't. Popular opinion is a mighty thing. The schoolgirls of to-day are the women of to-morrow, and the women of a country have an enormous amount to do with the formation of public opinion - more nowadays than ever before - and their influence will go on increasing with every year that passes. If each of us tries to help the world instead of hindering it, think what an asset each one may be to the country! It's really a tremendous honor to know that we can all take our part in the reconstruction of England. It's like each being allowed to lay a brick in the foundation of a new building. Of course you'll ask me: 'Well, and how are we going to help?' That's just what I want to talk about. We pride ourselves on being practical at the College. Some of us thought we might start a new society, to be called 'The Rainbow League.' It's a sort of 'Guild of Helpers,' and we want to do all kinds of jolly things to help in the town, something like our old 'Knitting Club' and 'Soldiers' Parcel Society,' only of course different. We could give concerts and make clothes for war orphans, and toys for the hospitals, and scrap-books for crippled children. There are heaps of nice things like that you'll just love doing. It's called 'The Rainbow League,' because a rainbow was set in the sky after the Flood, to help people to remember, and we want, in our small way, not to let the Great War be forgotten, but to do our bit to help with the future of the race.

"I'm not any great hand at speaking or explaining, so I want you each to take a copy of the rules of 'The Rainbow League' and to read them quietly over at home. Then any girl who likes to join can put her name down. All the Sixth want to become members, and I hope lots of others will too. That's all I have to say. I'm afraid I'm rather a bungler, but you'll understand everything if you read the papers. I'm going to give them out now."

Lispeth, very red in the face, came down from the platform, and, aided by her fellow-prefects, began to distribute papers right and left to the girls as they filed from the benches. Amongst the others, Ingred took hers, and put it in her pocket. She did not care to discuss it with the crowd, so retired to a corner of the hostel garden, and, amid a shower of falling autumn leaves, opened the typewritten sheet, and read as follows:

The Rainbow League

A Society for Schoolgirls who wish to help in the great work of reconstruction after the War

WHAT THE LEAGUE HOLDS

That every soul is of infinite and equal value, because all are the children of one Father.

That every girl must do her best to help all other girls, and to advance the Sisterhood of Women.

That woman's greatest and strongest weapons are love and sweetness.

That by conscious radiation of unselfish love to her fellow-beings, a girl may undoubtedly raise the moral atmosphere of the world around her.

That every girl, however young, can help this glorious old country, and that, joined together for good, the schoolgirls of a nation can influence the well-being of a race.

That good can always triumph over evil, and that love and unselfishness will wipe out many social blots, and put beauty in their place.

As the rainbow has seven prismatic colors, these may stand for seven talents of woman.

Violet = Virtue - the bed-rock of woman's influence.

Indigo = Industry - which means willing service.

Blue = Beauty - in its many and varied forms.

Green = Generosity - to give of our best to others.

Yellow = Youth - to offer our best years to God.

Orange = Order - which includes organization.

Red = Radiation - the Love Force going out to others.

Fellowship

Every member of the League shall pledge herself to forward its objects and to take an active part in any schemes of help that may be instituted in connection with it.

Flower Emblem. The Iris.

Motto. "Freely ye have received, freely give."

Ingred sat for a moment or two, watching the petals blow from the last roses on the bush that hung over the worn stone wall. The old Abbey lay on one hand, the buildings of the new school on the other. They seemed the very personification of ancient and modern.

"The world can't stand still," she thought, "and if it's got to move on, I suppose I'd better help to give it a shove in the right direction."

Walking into the hostel, she met Nora and Fil walking arm-in-arm.

"Hullo, Ingred! Have you read the paper about the Rainbow League?" asked Fil eagerly. "I think it's ripping! Nora and I are both going to join."

"And so am I," said Ingred, as she passed by them, and went upstairs.

# CHAPTER VII

## HOCKEY

Ingred signed her name next morning as a member of the Rainbow League, and received a neat notebook with a Japanese design of purple irisesstencilled on the cover. Though the new society was supposed to be run entirely by the girls themselves, it was much encouraged at head-quarters, and special allowances were made for its activities. Miss Burd sent for a book on *Toy-making at Home*, and gave the Handicraft classes an indulgence to concentrate for the present on the construction of little windmills, carts, dolls' furniture, trains, jigsaw puzzles, and other articles described in its fascinating pages. Such a number of girls had joined the League that many willing hands were at work, and at Christmas they hoped to have a sale of the best of the toys in aid of a fund for War Orphans, and to send the remainder to be given away as treats for poor children.

Lispeth was highly enthusiastic, and full of future schemes.

"We'll do toy-making this term," she decreed, "and then next term we can think of something else. In the spring and summer we'll have a Posy Union to send bunches of flowers to sick people. We can't do anything of that, of course, during the winter, unless some of you like to put down bulbs; it would be lovely to give a pot of purple crocuses to a little crippled child! I think making the toys is just A1. I want to start a manufactory!"

"Barring the glue," said Susie Wakefield. "It smells simply abominable when it boils over. Why doesn't somebody bring out a patent for sweet-scented glue?"

"Sweet-scented glue! You Sybarite!"

"Why not? They could make it out of all those delicious gums and resins you read about in books on the Spice Islands, instead of - by the by, what is glue made of?"

"Horses' hoofs, I believe, but I fancy it's better not to ask what it's made of. I don't think your gums and resins would do the deed so well. We'd best stick to good old-fashioned glue."

"That's just what I complained of - I *do* stick to it, or rather it sticks to me. I get it all over my hands, and smears down my overall."

"Then you're an untidy workwoman, old sport, and I can't do anything for you except recommend 'Gresolvent.'"

The girls were grateful for the latitude of the Handicraft class, for otherwise they would have had little or no time to give to the construction of toys. The homework of the College was stiff, and certain games were compulsory. The hockey season had begun, and fixtures had been made with other schools in the neighborhood.

"We must see that the old Coll. keeps up its reputation," said Blossom Webster, the games captain. "Last year, when we had Lennie Peters and Sophy Aston, we did a thing or two, didn't we? 'What girl has done, girl can do!' and we've just got to buck up and try."

"Rather!" agreed the team.

Among the various matches which had been arranged was one with The Clinton High School Old Girls' Association. It was an amateur team of enthusiasts, who, debarred from playing any longer for their school, had established a club of their own. They had sent a challenge to Grovebury College, and it had been accepted.

"Saturday morning's a weird time for a match!" said Blossom, re-reading the letter to her chums. "But their captain says it's the only time they can get their field. It's used by another club in the afternoons, so she's fixed eleven o'clock."

"It suits me rather decently," said Janie Potter. "I'm going out to tea in the afternoon, so I couldn't have come if the match had been at three. Don't stare at me like that! *No* I'm *not* a slacker! I must accept invitations to tea sometimes, even if I *am* in the team. What a dragon you are, Blossom!"

"Good thing some one keeps the team up, or you'd be gadding off tea-drinking instead of playing!" returned Blossom grimly. "Grovebury expects every girl to do her duty on Saturday. It will be bad luck for the season if we lose our first match."

The Clinton Old Girls' Association had its field at Denscourt, a town ten miles away from Grovebury. It was arranged by the team, and for any girls from the college who cared to come as spectators, to meet at the railway station at 10:15, and travel together under the escort of Miss Giles.

Ingred, who was a keen player, and very proud of having been placed in the reserve, was to spend Friday night at the hostel, instead of returning as usual to Wynch-on-the-Wold.

Nora, Verity, and Fil were also to be numbered among the spectators.

On the eventful morning, as the girls were just finishing breakfast, a telegram arrived for Rachel Grant. She tore open the yellow envelope, and her face fell as she read the brief message. Her mother was seriously ill, and she must return home immediately. Mrs. Best went upstairs at once to arrange for her hurried journey, and to help her to pack.

Downstairs at the breakfast-table the girls discussed the bad news. They were very sorry for Rachel, and also for themselves, for she was their right inner.

"It's like our luck!" fretted Janie Potter.

"Too disgusting for words!" groused Doreen Hayward.

"Poor old Rachel!" groaned Fil.

"What's going to be done?" asked everybody, as they folded their serviettes and left the table.

That question was answered by Miss Giles, who beckoned to Ingred in the hall, and said briefly:

"Ingred, will you fetch your hockey-stick and pads?"

Ingred did not need telling twice. To take Rachel's place was indeed an honor. Such a chance did not come often. With huge satisfaction she donned her neat navy-blue skirt, edged with its orange band, and her blouse with its orange collar and cuffs.

"You lucker!" sighed Nora enviously. "I'd just jolly well give everything I have to be in the match to-day. It's not much sport to stand by and cheer. Oh, don't think I'm trying to get out of coming! I'm going to look on and see that you do your duty. If you're not playing up, I'll hiss!"

"I'll do my best," laughed Ingred, "and if I drop down for sheer lack of breath, I shall expect you and Verity to carry me home. There!"

"Right you are! It's a bargain, though you'd be a jolly heavy burden, I can tell you."

The team, Miss Giles, and about twenty girls as spectators, were punctual to their appointment, and assembled at the station just in time for the train. By a little maneuvering, combined with good fortune, they secured three compartments to themselves, for a solitary old gentleman, whom they found in possession of a corner seat, bolted in alarm at such an invasion of schoolgirls, and sought sanctuary in a smoking carriage. Some generous spirits had brought chocolates and butter-scotch, which they shared round, and Nora, the irrepressible, produced from her pocket a mouth-organ, with which she proceeded to entertain the company, until frantic raps from the next compartment made her aware that Miss Giles heard and disapproved of her amateur recital. Naturally the talk was largely about hockey and the chances of the match. It was known that the Old Clintonians were a strong team, for most of them had been the crack players of their school. To beat them would indeed be a feather in the cap of the college.

"Too good to come off!" groaned Blossom gloomily.

"Nonsense, you can't tell till you've tried! Make up your mind you're going to win!" said Nora indignantly. "I shan't speak to you again if you lose this match!"

"I'm only one out of eleven, please!"

"Well, I don't care! One who makes up her mind to fail can spoil everything, and vice-versa, so just buck up and win!"

The hockey ground was not very far from the station at Denscourt, and when the Grovebury contingent arrived they found the Old Clintonians ready and waiting for them. The eleven ran into the pavilion and took off the long coats that had covered their gym costumes; then trooped out on to the field, as neat and business-like looking a team as could be imagined. Blossom, with her chums, Janie and Doreen, took good stock of their opponents.

"They're a strong set, and will take some beating," said Janie.

"Rather!" agreed Blossom. "You may be sure we're not going to goal just when we please."

"They look topping sports!" commented Doreen.

Everything was now in perfect order; the teams were placed, and the umpire blew her whistle for the match to begin. As the account of such a contest is always much more interesting when narrated by an actual spectator, and as Nora wrote a long and accurate description of it afterwards to a cousin at school in London, I will insert her letter, and allow it to speak for itself.

(*This letter is an account of a real match, written by a real schoolgirl.*)

"Grovebury College.

"*My Dear Margaret,*

"I simply must tell you about the hockey match we played last Saturday!

"The team played the Clinton High School Old Girls' Association at Denscourt. Our girls were awfully keen to meet them, and were not at all daunted by the fact that they were exceptionally strong.

"About twenty of us went as spectators, and as we were about to set off to the station with the Eleven, Rachel Grant, the Left Inner, received a telegram, conveying news of her mother's serious illness. To our great misfortune, she was obliged to go home at once, and the first girl on the Reserve, Ingred Saxon, had to fill her place.

"Miss Giles, the Games Mistress, went on to get the tickets, and, in spite of some delay, we managed to meet her in time to catch the train. It is ten miles from here to Denscourt, and we arrived there in about twenty minutes.

"The field is not very far from the railway station. The team girls were taken to the pavilion, and when they were ready, the captain tossed up. Veronica Hall, the opposing captain, who is a tall strong girl, and a fine hockey player, won the toss, and chose to play against the wind for the first half. At exactly eleven, the center forwards, Blossom and Veronica, began the bully-off. There were three dull clashes as their sticks met, and then with a dexterous stroke, Blossom passed the ball to her Right Inner, Janie Potter. Before she could strike, the wing on the opposite side captured the ball, and with a clean drive sent it spinning down the field. It was soon stopped, however, by Doreen Hayward, the Right Half, who, after successfully dribbling it past the enemy Inner, sent it hard out to Aline West, the School Right Wing. Soon Aline had the ball half-way up the field, but suddenly she stumbled, and fell headlong to the ground. Before she could rise, the ball had been sent to the rival Center Forward, who, with a magnificent hit, drove it nearly into the goal-circle. There it was splendidly blocked by Kitty Saunders, our Left Back, and quickly passed to Evie Irving, the Left Wing. There was a brief, though fierce, struggle for possession of the ball between the two wings, in which Evie was victorious. She neatly avoided the Clinton Right Half, but the ball went off the line. The opposing Half-back rolled in - to her wing, as she thought - but with a swift movement, Ingred Saxon, the Left Inner, reached the ball first, and taking it with her, ran up the field like lightning. The Inner on the other side was an equally fast runner, but Ingred easily evaded her opponent's continued efforts to get the ball for some time.

"'Oh! has she lost the ball?' 'No. Is she still flying on, the ball before her?' 'Will she pass the rival back safely?' were the questions which thronged my brain, nearly paralyzed with excitement.

"Not able to dribble the ball any farther, and being attacked by a girl wearing the Clinton colors, Ingred hit the ball out to her wing, who struck in to center again. The Left Back on the opposing side stopped it just as it entered the goal-circle.

"'Clear!' yelled one of the onlookers, unable to contain herself, and with a fine stroke the Back sent the ball flying away to the other side of the field. It went with such force that, although our Right Back made an attempt to stop it, it raced past her stick and over the outside line. After the roll-in, nearly all the play was carried on practically in the center of the field. Each side displayed some excellent passing, but when the whistle blew at half time, neither had scored. By this time all the girls were hot and panting, except the Goal-keepers, and were ready for the brief rest. Our Eleven stood in a group together, sharing the lemons which the Clinton girls provided, and discussing the events of the last half-hour.

"'Girls!' exclaimed Blossom, our captain 'we simply must win this match! We shall have the wind against us the next half, but we are not going to let things end in a victory for the Clintonians, or in a draw either, are we?'

"'No!' was the decided answer.

"A few minutes later every one was in her place again, but of course defending the other goal. Blossom and Veronica were once more bullying-off. This time the latter was the quicker of the two, for, with a clever hit, she succeeded in sending the ball away to her Left Wing. The Clinton Left Wing began to dribble it along towards the goal we were defending, and, when confronted by our Right Half, passed it to her center. I almost screamed out to our Center Forward not to let Veronica keep the ball, for I knew she was a dangerous opponent. She was well up the field, and with a neat turn of her stick sent the ball past our Right Back. There was only one girl now to prevent her from getting a goal! Blossom was now fast gaining, and then, just as Veronica came within shooting distance, her foot slipped in the slimy mud, and she lost her balance.

Blossom was level with Veronica by this time, and before the Clinton captain could steady herself, she had sent the ball far away from the danger zone.

"The play went on fairly evenly again until five minutes to twelve. I felt wild with anxiety, and I am sure the others did too, for there were only five minutes left.

"The ball had just been sent over the line by one of the Clinton girls, and our Left Half rolled in. The wing missed the bill, but Ingred took it, and - well, I cannot tell you clearly what happened after that. I still have in my mind the picture of Ingred, who, the ball at her side, literally flew up the field, her feet scarcely touching the ground. No one knows how she did it, but by some marvellous playing she passed all her opponents, and shot the only goal of the whole match just three seconds before the whistle blew for 'Time.'

"Of course Ingred was the heroine of the hour. As she was being escorted to the pavilion, flushed but triumphant, Miss Giles said to her: 'Well played! I am proud of you!'

"Those few words of praise meant a good deal to Ingred, and we all felt how well she deserved them, especially as it was only by accident that she played in the team at all.

"I do hope I have not tired you by going too fully into our match, but I know you are interested in our school games, hockey in particular. I will tell you about our later fixtures when I see you at Christmas, so until then - Good-bye.

"With love from your affectionate cousin,

"Nora Clifford."

# CHAPTER VIII

## AN UNPLEASANT EXPERIENCE

The girls filed out from the hockey ground as speedily as possible. There was a train due from Grovebury in about a quarter of an hour. They walked to the station in groups, discussing details of the match as they went. Ingred, Beatrice, and Verity happened to be blocked at the exit by the Clintonian team, and were obliged to wait some minutes before they could pass, and when at last they were through the gate, all their own schoolfellows were disappearing up the road.

"We needn't run after them - I believe we've plenty of time," said Verity. "We can almost see the station from here. I say, aren't you fearfully hungry? I'm literally starving. Let's find a confectioner's and each buy a bun before we go."

Both Beatrice and Ingred felt that they required fortifying before they started for home, so they dived into the nearest pastry-cook's and demanded buns. They were eating them rather hastily, when Linda Slater entered the shop in company with a gentleman, evidently her father. She hailed he classmates, and at once began to talk over the match and rejoice at the school victory.

"Who says we're no good at games now? This has sent up our credit ten per cent! I'm proud of the Coll.!"

"Blossom was A1," exulted Verity.

Angela Brazil

"And Janie was simply ripping. Dad thought no end of her. Didn't you, Dad?"

"Well, I'm glad we made something of a record," admitted Ingred.

"I say," declared Beatrice, hastily finishing her bun, "if that clock's right, we must bolt for our train."

"As a matter of fact, it's one minute slow," exclaimed Linda, consulting her watch. "You'll have to sprint."

"Aren't *you* coming?"

"No, we have our car here. It's outside."

"Those girls will hardly catch their train," remarked Mr. Slater to Linda, as the three went to the pay desk to settle for their buns. "Couldn't we stow them into the car, and take them along with us?"

"Oh, no, Dad!" frowned Linda. "There really isn't room. You promised you'd call at Brantbury and bring Gerald and Eustace back for the afternoon. We couldn't cram them all in the car!"

"There isn't time for them to get the train."

"Oh, yes! You don't know how they can run!"

Quite unaware of the kindly offer which had been rejected on their behalf, Beatrice, Verity, and Ingred fled from the shop, and hurried with all possible speed in the direction of the railway station. They could see the train coming along the top of the embankment, and it had drawn up at the platform before they reached the passenger entrance. They were not the only late comers. It was Saturday, and a crowd of work people from various factories near were returning to Grovebury.

In company with a very mixed and motley crew they pushed their way up the long flight of steps. A collector stood at the top, and just as they were nearing their goal, he slammed the gate and refused further admission to the platform. They could hear the whistle, and the general bumping of chains that betokened the starting of the carriages. They were exactly half a minute too late! When the train was well out of the station, the collector once more opened his barrier, and the crowd surged on. The three girls, who disliked pushing among a rough assembly, stood on one side to let the people pass by. There was no hurry now, and no object to be gained by forcing their way ahead. Last of all, therefore, they presented themselves at the gate.

"Tickets, please!" repeated the collector automatically.

All three felt in their pockets, but felt in vain. Return tickets and purses were alike missing, and even penknives and handkerchiefs had vanished, Ingred's pocket, indeed, was neatly turned inside out. Here was a dilemma! They had evidently been robbed on the stairs by a professional thief, who had appropriated all their portable belongings. In utter consternation they looked at one another.

"We've lost our tickets!" faltered Beatrice.

"They've been stolen!" added Ingred.

"Do please let us through!" entreated Verity.

In ordinary circumstanced the collector would no doubt have listened to the girl's story, and taken them to interview the station-master, but to-day he had to do double duty, and could scarcely cope with the extra work. He had to deal with crowds, and to keep a sharp eye to see that no one defrauded the railway company by travelling without paying the fare. A train was due at the next moment on the other side of the platform, and his services were urgently required at the opposite exit.

"Haven't you got your tickets?" he demanded curtly. "Then I must close the gate. No one's allowed on the platform without tickets."

The advancing train whistled as it ran through the cutting, and, disregarding the girls' remonstrances, the official locked the barrier. He bolted across the line in front of the engine, just in time to take his place at the other gateway before the rush of passengers began, and probably never gave another thought to the three whom he had just excluded. Left shut out on the top of the station steps, the unlucky trio ruefully reviewed the situation.

"What *are* we to do?" demanded Ingred breathlessly.

"Goodness only knows!" sighed Verity.

"We're in a very awkward fix!" admitted Beatrice.

They were much too far from Grovebury to make walking possible.

"I wonder Miss Giles didn't miss us!" fretted Verity, trying to throw the blame on somebody.

"It isn't her fault - fair play to her!" urged Beatrice. "She wasn't looking after us officially to-day, you know. On Saturdays we're supposed to be on our own."

"I lay the blame on buns!" said Ingred. "We'd have kept with the rest of the school if we hadn't stopped at that confectioner's."

"Well, it's no use crying over spilt milk now! What we've got to do is to find some means of getting home. We can't stay here all day."

"I believe it's not very far to Waverley from Denscourt," ventured Beatrice. "If we can manage to walk, I know some people who live at a house there. I'd ask them to lend us our fares, and we could catch a train at Waverley station."

The idea seemed feasible, and, as it was the only one that suggested itself, they unanimously decided to adopt it. They walked down the steps again, therefore, on to the high road, and, stopping a girl who was passing, asked the way to Waverley.

"It's a good four miles by the road, but it's only about two by the fields," she volunteered in reply. "I think you'd find the path. You go down the road to the right, and turn through the first gate across a field to a farm. Then you keep along the river bank, on the left. You can't miss it."

To save two miles in their present predicament was a matter of importance, and they all felt that they would greatly prefer walking through fields to tramping along a dusty high road. Thanking their informant, they took her advice, and set off in the direction which she indicated. After all, the affair was rather an adventure.

"The Mortons are sure to offer us lunch when we get there," affirmed Beatrice; "of course we shall be fearfully late home, and our people will be getting very anxious about us, but we can't help that. I was to have gone to a matinee of *Carmen* this afternoon, but it's off, naturally! I expect Doris will use my ticket, when I don't turn up."

"I meant to wash our dog when I got back!" laughed Ingred. "He'll have to look dirty on Sunday, now."

"And I meant to do a hundred things; but what's the use of talking about them now?" groaned Verity. "Here's our farm, and that appears to be the river over there. Didn't that girl say: 'Keep along to the left'? Perhaps we'd better ask again."

They verified their instructions from a boy who was standing in the farmyard, whittling a stick, and trudged away over a stubble field and through a turnstile gate. It was quite pretty along the path by the river. There was a tall hedge where hips and haws showed red, and a grassy border where a few wild flowers still bloomed. The sun shed a soft golden autumnal haze over the fields and bushes and the li nes ofyellow trees.

The girls rather enjoyed themselves; it was an unexpected country excursion, and had all the charm of novelty. They walked about half a mile, chatting about school matters as they went, then suddenly they were confronted by an alternative. A bridge spanned the river, and the broad, well-trodden path along which they had come turned over the bridge. There was indeed a track that continued along the left bank, but it was over-grown, and looked little used. Which were they to take?

That was a question which required discussion.

"The girl said: 'keep along the river bank on the left,'" urged Ingred.

"Yet the path so plainly goes across here," demurred Verity.

"That's certainly the left bank, but that way looks as if it led to nowhere," vacillated Beatrice.

"Can't we ask anybody?"

"There isn't a soul in sight."

"Isn't there a signpost?"

"Nothing of the sort."

"Then which way *shall* we go?"

"Better take votes on it."

"Right-o! I'm for 'bypath meadow.'"

"And I'm for the 'king's highway.'"

"So am I, so we're two to one!"

"I'll give in, then," said Ingred, "only I've a sort of feeling we're going wrong, all the same!"

The new path led along the opposite bank, and was very much a replica of the former. It ran on and on for what seemed quite a long distance, but they met nobody from whom they could inquire the way. For nearly a quarter of a mile a belt of trees obscured the view, and when at last the prospect could once more be seen, Beatrice stopped short with a groan of despair. On the other side of the water was the unmistakable spire of Waverley church.

"We've come wrong, after all!"

"Oh, good night! So we have!"

"What an absolute swindle!"

The girls were certainly not in luck that day. They had missed their path as effectually as they had missed their train. The chimneys of Waverley were in sight, but separated from them by a wide stream, and unless they were prepared to wade, swim, or fly, there was no way of reaching the village.

"There's nothing for it but to turn back!"

"Why, but that's *miles*!"

"Are you sure it's Waverley over there? Can we ask anybody?"

"No one to ask, worse luck!"

"Yes, there is! I can see some people coming along in a boat."

Rendered desperate by the emergency, Ingred struggled

Angela Brazil

through the reeds to the very edge of the river, and lifted up her voice in an agonized cry of "Help!"

A punt was drifting slowly with the current, and its occupants, a lady and gentleman, looked with surprise at the agitated girl who was hailing them from the bank. The gentleman at once paddled in her direction, and, running his little craft among the reeds, inquired what was the matter.

"Oh, please, is that Waverley over there?" asked Ingred anxiously. "We've lost our way, and we've walked miles! Is there any bridge near?"

"That's certainly Waverley, but there's no bridge till you come to one a mile and a half down stream."

Ingred's face was tragic. She turned to Beatrice and Verity, who had joined her.

"It's no use! We shall have to go back!"

But the lady was whispering something to the gentleman, and he beckoned to the girls with a smile.

"Don't run away!" he said. "Look here, we'll punt you across if you like."

"Like!" The girls hardly knew how to express their gratitude.

"The three of you'd be too heavy a load. I think I'd better take just one at a time. Can you manage to get in? It's rather swampy here. Give me your hand!"

Ingred splashed ankle deep in oozy mud as she scrambled on board, but that was a trifle compared with the relief of being ferried over the river. Her knight-errant was neither young nor handsome, being, indeed, rather bald and stout, but no orthodox interesting hero of fiction could have been more welcome at the moment. She tendered her utmost thanks as she landed, again with damage to her shoes, on the rushy bank opposite. Their friends in need, having successfully punted over Beatrice and Verity also, bade them a laughing good-bye, and resumed their easy course down stream, leaving three very grateful girls behind the m.

"That's helped us out of a fix! Don't say again we've no luck!" cried Beatrice, wiping her boots carefully on the grass.

"They were angels in disguise!" sighed Ingred.

"Rather stout angels!" chuckled Verity. "Now, how are we going to get out of this field?"

"Over the hedge, I suppose. There's a piece of fence that looks climbable!" returned Beatrice, swinging herself up with elephantine grace, and dropping with a heavy thud on the other side. "Oh! good biz! We're on a cinder path!"

They were indeed in a back lane which led at the bottom of some gardens, then behind a row of stables, and finally through a gate on to the high road.

"I know where we are now!" exclaimed Beatrice gleefully. "It's only quite a short way to the Morton's. They live in the next terrace but two. I believe we're within measurable distance of some lunch."

This was such good news that they strode along in renewed spirits. Considering all, they thought the adventure was turning out well. A meal would undoubtedly be most acceptable, if Beatrice's friends were hospitable enough to offer it.

"It's the fourth house," said Beatrice, "the one with the copper beech over the gate. Linden Lea - yes, here we are! Oh, I say, what are all the blinds down for?"

The girls faced each other blankly.

"Is anyone dead?" faltered Ingred.

"I'll ring and inquire, at any rate," murmured Beatrice.

So she rang, and rang again and yet again. She could hear the bell clanging quite plainly and unmistakably somewhere in the back regions, yet nobody came to the door.

"It's funny! I don't hear anybody in the house either," she remarked. "Their dog generally barks at the least sound."

At that moment a small face peeped over the top of the wall which divided the garden from that of the next house, and a childish voice asked:

"Do you want the Mortons?"

"Yes. Isn't anybody in?"

"They're all gone away to Llandudno, for a month."

"All? Isn't anyone here?"

"No, the house is locked up."

Here a warning call of "Willie!" caused their informant to disappear as suddenly as he had come, but the girls had heard enough. All their hopes were suddenly blighted. They had arrived at the end of their journey only to draw a blank. They were indeed in a worse position than when they had missed the train at Denscourt, for they were farther from home, and it was much later. Almost ready to cry, they turned down the garden again.

"We've got to get home to-night somehow!" said Ingred through her set teeth.

"Shall we go to the police station?" quavered Verity.

"And give ourselves up like lost children? No, it's too undignified! Wait a moment, I've got an idea!" said Beatrice. "We passed the post office just now, and I noticed it had a 'Public Telephone.' I'll ring up Mother and tell her where we are, and ask her to come over for us."

"But you can't telephone for nothing, and we haven't so much as a solitary penny amongst us!"

"I know. I thought I'd explain that to the people at the post office, and ask them to let me have the call, and Mother will pay when she comes. I could give them my watch as a security."

"It's worth trying!"

So, with just a little grain of hope, they retraced their steps to the post office, which was also a stationer's and newsagent's. Nobody was in the shop, but when the girls thumped on the counter a rosy-cheeked young person appeared from the back regions.

"Want to telephone without paying? It's against the post office rules," she snapped, as Beatrice briefly explained the circumstances.

"My mother will pay when she comes, and if you'd take my watch -"

"I can't go against post office rules! All calls must be paid for beforehand. That's our instructions."

"But just for once -"

"What's the matter, Doris?" asked a voice, and a kindly-looking little man emerged from the back parlor, wiping his mouth hastily, and took his place behind the counter. Beatrice turned to him with eagerness, and again stated the urgency of their peculiar situation.

Angela Brazil

"Well, of course we've our instructions from the post office, and we've got to account for the calls, but in this particular case we might let you have one, and pay afterwards," he replied. "Oh, never mind the watch; it's all right!"

Beatrice lost no time in ringing up Number 167 Grovebury, and to her immense delight, when she got the connection, she heard her mother's voice at the instrument. A short explanation was all that was necessary.

"Stay where you are at the Waverley post office, and I will get a taxi and fetch you myself immediately," returned Mrs. Jackson. "It's the greatest relief to know what has become of you. I was going to ring up the police station, and describe you as 'missing!'"

The girls had to wait nearly three-quarters of an hour before the taxi made its appearance, and the welcome form of Mrs. Jackson stepped out of it. She paid what was owing for the call, thanked the postmaster for his civility, and hustled the girls into the conveyance as quickly as possible.

"I suppose girls will be girls," she said, "but I think you've been very silly ones to-day! Why didn't you keep with the rest of the school, as you ought to have done?"

"It sounds a most horrible greedy confession," replied Beatrice guiltily, "but I'm afraid it was all the fault of - buns! They just threw us late, and we missed the others. We'll never buy buns again! Never! Never! *O peccavi!* We have sinned!"

And she looked so humorously contrite that Mrs. Jackson, who was inclined to scold, laughed in spite of herself, and forgave the delinquents.

"On condition that such a thing doesn't happen again!" she declared.

"Trust us! We wouldn't go through such an experience again

for all the buns in the world! Next time we'll cling to the College apron strings like - like -"

"Like adhesive sticking-plaster!" supplied Ingred gently.

"Or oysters to a mermaid's tail!" murmured Verity.

Angela Brazil

# CHAPTER IX

## A HOSTEL FROLIC

"The Foursome League," which Verity had instituted with her room-mates at the hostel, was kept by them as a solemn compact. They stuck to one another nobly, though often in the teeth of great inconvenience. It generally took three of them to urge Fil through her toilet in the mornings and drag her down to breakfast in time. She was always so terribly sleepy at seven o'clock, and so positive that she could whisk through her dressing in ten minutes, and that it was quite unnecessary to get up so soon: even when the others mercilessly pulled the bed-clothes from her, and pointed to their watches, she would dawdle instead of "whisking," and spend much superfluous time over manicure or dabbing on cucumber cream to improve her complexion. She was so innocent about her little vanities, and conducted them with such child-like complacency, that the girls tolerated them quite good humoredly, and even assisted sometimes. One of them generally volunteered to brush her long flaxen hair, and tie her ribbon, and half out of habit the others would tidy her cubicle, which was apt to be chaotic, and put her things away in her drawers. They did it almost automatically, for they had come to look upon Fil somewhat in the light of a big doll, the exclusive property of "The Foursome League," and to be treated as the mascot of the dormitory.

Mrs. Best, the hostel matron, was what the girls called "rather an old dear." Her gray hair was picturesque, and the knowledge that she had lost her husband and a son in the war added an element of pathetic interest to her personality. She was experienced in the ways of girls, and contrived to keep order without seeming to be constantly obtruding rules. Among her various sane practices she instituted the plan of awarding marks for good conduct and order to each dormitory, and allowing the one which scored the highest to give an entertainment to the others during the last hour before bedtime on Thursday night. Naturally this was a privilege to be desired. It was fun to act variety artistes before the rest of the hostel, and well worth being in time for meals, preserving silence during prep., or getting up a little earlier so as to leave cubicles in apple-pie order. The Foursome League had not yet earned distinction, chiefly owing to lapses on the part of Fil, and Nora's incorrigible love of talking in season and out of season. One week, however, after a really heroic series of efforts, they succeeded in establishing a record, and sat perking themselves at dinner-time when Mrs. Best read out the score.

"We've not had you on the boards before," said Susie Wakefield, one of the Sixth, as the girls filed from the room when the meal was over; "we're all expecting something extra tiptop and thrillsome, so play up!"

"Hope we shan't let you down!" replied Ingred. "Please don't expect too much, or you mayn't get it!"

Dormitory 2 held a hurried conclave before afternoon school.

"It's a great stunt!" rejoiced Nora.

"What *are* we to act?" fluttered Fil.

"Especially when we've to play up!" twittered Verity.

"What silly idiots we were not to plan it all out beforehand! But I really never dreamt we'd ever get the chance!"

"No more did I," said Ingred, sitting with her head in her

Angela Brazil

hands, considering. "On the whole, it doesn't matter. Sometimes a quite impromptu thing goes off best. It's largely a question of what costumes we can rake up out of nothing.

"The cleverer those are, the more we'll get applauded. I've one or two ideas simmering. Thank goodness it's drawing this afternoon, and I shall have time to think them over."

"We'll all think!" agreed Verity. "Then we'll compare notes at four o'clock, and fix on what we're going to do. Great Minerva! It'll be a hectic evening! I'm shivering in my shoes!"

"And I'm absolutely green with stage-fright! What a life!" proclaimed Fil.

If Miss Godwin, the drawing-mistress, noticed a slacking off in accuracy on the part of four of her pupils, that afternoon, she perhaps set it down to want of artistic feeling. It is difficult to copy with absolute exactness when only your fingers are busy, and your brain is far away. Ingred planned enough entertainments to supply a Pierrot troupe for a month, but abandoned most of them as being quite impossible to act with the very limited resources that were available at the hostel. At a select Foursome Committee after school, however, she presented the pick of the performances, and as nobody else had thought of anything better, or indeed quite so good, her suggestions, with a few amendments and alterations, were carried unanimously.

At eight o'clock that evening, when preparation was finished, the boarders' room was rapidly transformed into an amateur theater. The trestle tables were carried to one end to form the gallery, rows of chairs represented the dress circle, and cushions in front either the pit or the stalls, according to individual taste, or, as Mrs. Best said, the behavior of the occupants.

There was no curtain, but, as the scenery preserved Shakespearian methods of simplicity, that did not matter. Part of the charm of these Thursday night entertainments was their absolutely spontaneous character, and the fact that many details had to be left to the imagination of the spectators only made things more amusing.

When the audience, after a slight struggle for gallery seats, had settled itself, and Mrs. Best and Nurse Warner had taken possession of the arm-chairs specially reserved for them, Dollie Ransome, who had been requisitioned by the performers to act as Greek chorus, placed some stools by the fire-place, and announced importantly:

"King Alfred and the Cakes. A Historical Drama."

The little old woman who entered, carrying some sticks and a basin, was difficult to identify as Fil. Her fair hair had been powdered, wrinkles were painted on her smooth forehead, a handkerchief was knotted on her head for a cap, and she wore an apron borrowed from the cook, and a check table-cover arranged as a shawl. She bestowed the sticks in the fender to represent a fire on the hearth, and taking some biscuits from her basin, placed them amongst the supposed embers, indulging meanwhile in a soliloquy about the hardness of the times for poor folk, and the danger from the Danes.

A violent knocking on the door was followed by the entrance of such a magnificent object that the spectators immediately applauded his advent. Nora, with her large build, short-cut hair, and generally boyish appearance, was the very one to act King Alfred. She had folded a plaid traveling rug into a kilt which reached just to her bare knees, borrowed a velvet coatee and a leather belt from Mrs. Best, and, by the aid of bandages from the ambulance cupboard, had made quite a good imitation of Saxon leg-gear. Armed with a bow and arrows, hastily constructed from twigs cut in the garden, she advanced with a manly stride, begged for hospitality, and was accommodated with a stool by the hearth, where she sat whittling arrows in an abstracted fashion, and heaving gusty sighs.

Angela Brazil

The audience had hardly recovered from its astonishment when it was thrilled again by the entrance of an ancient and elderly peasant man, so disguised that it was almost impossible to recognize Ingred. A water-proof with a broad leather belt served as coat, and, being padded inside with a pillow, gave the effect of bent and bowed shoulders. Some tow, supplied by Mrs. Best, was fastened as a long straggling beard, and bushy eyebrows of the same material were fixed on with soap. Leaning heavily upon a stick, he came limping in, complaining in a tremulous voice of his rheumatism, started with amazement at the sight of the handsome stranger seated by his hearth, and drew his wife aside for explanations. The old couple, after conversing in audible whispers, decided to go out for more firewood, and as a last charge the dame commended her cakes to the care of their guest. King Alfred, on being left alone by the hearth, whittled away at his arrows with more energy than discrimination, and showed indeed a sad lack of practical skill for so well seasoned a warrior. Perhaps, however, he was not accustomed to have to make them for himself, and missed his chief archer. Throwing them down at last, he sank his head in his hands in an absolute cinema pose of despondency, and sighed to an extent which must have been painful to his lungs. The dame returned to sniff burning cakes and fly to the rescue of her cookery. Fil was quite a good little actress, and produced what she considered her *piece de resistance*. She had spent her summer holidays in Somerset, and had there picked up a local ballad which dealt with the legend in dialect. She brought out a verse of it now with great effect:

"Cusn't ee zee the ca-akes, man?
And cusn't ee zee 'em burrn?
I'se warrant ee eat 'em fast enough,
Zoon as it be ee turn!"

And catching up a biscuit, carefully blackened beforehand by toasting it over the gas, she flaunted it in the face of the embarrassed monarch.

The dramatic situation was slightly spoilt by the delay in the entrance of the courtier, who ought to have come in at that psychological moment, and didn't. The fact was that Verity, finding it dull waiting in the passage, had run upstairs to make some additions to her costume, and had miscalculated the length, or rather shortness, of the act. It is difficult for the most accomplished actor to go on looking embarrassed for any length of time, and as Fil's eloquence in the scolding line suddenly failed her, there was an awful pause while the peasant husband, with wonderful agility considering his rheumatism, hopped to the door and called agitatedly for the missing performer. The courtier flew downstairs like a whirlwind, tripped into the room, and fell upon his red-stockinged knees to do homage to his sovereign, who rose majestically and extended a hand of pardon to the now grovelling peasant.

The audience, particularly that portion seated in the gallery, clapped and cheered to such an extent that one of the trestles, which had been carelessly fixed, collapsed, and sent a whole row of girls sliding on to the floor, whence they were rescued speechless with laughter, but uninjured. They came crowding round the performers to admire the costumes.

"They're topping!"

"How *did* you think of them?"

"I like King Alfred's legs!"

"Ingred, you look about a hundred!"

"Fil *could* scold!"

"Verity, what was a courtier doing rambling about a forest in a blue dressing-gown? It would get torn on the bushes!"

"I know. We told her so, but she *would* wear it!" declared Ingred. "She was just pig-headed over that dressing-gown!"

"Well, go and look at the Saxon pictures for yourself, in the history book!" retorted Verity, sticking to her point. "You'll see the courtiers in long flowing garments very like dressing-gowns. I think it was a capital idea, and the best I could do. There wasn't another rug for the kilt anyhow, and when other people have taken the best parts and the nicest costumes, you've just got to put up with anything you can find that's left."

"You did it so well," Ingred assured her hastily, for Verity had gone very pink, and her voice sounded distinctly offended. "I thought the way you dropped on one knee and cried: 'My liege lord! I am your humble socman!' was most impressive. What made you think of 'socman'?"

"Got it out of the history book," said Verity, slightly mollified. "It means a man who owned land, but wasn't quite as high up as a thane. I meant to bring in some more Saxon words, but I hadn't time."

"You must win the dormitory score again, and give us another performance," urged Mrs. Best. "I'm afraid it's too late for any more to-night, though we're all sorry to stop. Those juniors ought to be in bed. Janie and Doreen, if you'd like a quiet half-hour to finish your prep. you may go into my room. Somebody put the tables back, please, and be sure the trestles are in their right places this time, we don't want another collapse! Phyllis, your cough's worse. Nurse shall rub your chest with camphorated oil, and you mustn't kiss anybody. Betty too? I'll give you a lozenge, but don't suck it lying down in bed, in case you choke."

So saying, Mrs. Best, who generally mothered the hostel, dismissed her large family and bustled away with Nurse to superintend the putting to bed of the juniors and the due care of those who might be regarded as even ever so slightly on the sick list. It was perhaps owing to the excitement of their spirited performance that the members of No. 2 Dormitory could not get to sleep that night. They all lay wide awake in bed, and told each other tales about burglars, in whispers.

Verity's stories were blood-curdling in the extreme; she was a great reader, and had got them from magazines. Her three room-mates listened with cold shivers running down their spines. According to Verity's accounts it was a common and every day occurrence for a house-breaker to force an entrance, murder the occupants, and depart, leaving a case to baffle the police until some amateur detective turned up and solved the mystery.

"Has it ever struck you that the hostel would be a very easy place to burgle?" asked Fil. "Those French windows have no shutters, and the glass could be cut with a diamond."

"Or the doors could be opened with a skeleton key!" quavered Nora.

"I suppose they generally wear goloshes, so as to tread softly," ventured Ingred.

"Wouldn't it be dreadful," continued Verity, whose mind still ran on magazine stories, "to marry a fascinating man whom you'd met by chance, and then find out that he was a gentleman-burglar? What would you do?"

"It often happens on the cinema," said Nora. "The girl wavers about in an agony whether to tell or not, and wrings her hands and rolls her eyes, like they always *do* roll them on the films, and then, just when things are at the very last gasp, the husband tumbles over a precipice, or is wrecked at sea, or smashed in a railway accident, and she marries the other, who's as good as gold, and loved her first."

"Is the man who loves you first always as good as gold?" asked Fil.

"Well, generally on the Pictures. He's loved you as a child, you see. You come on the film hand in hand, in socks, and he gives you his apple."

"But suppose they don't love you from a child?" said Fil plaintively. "I've only known a lot of horrid little boys whom I didn't care for in the least. None of them ever gave me his apple, though I remember one taking mine. Is the first fascinating man I meet the true lover or the burglar? How am I to know which is which?"

"You'd better let me be there to decide for you, child, or you'll be snapped up by the first adventurer that comes along," declared Nora. "Don't trust him if he has a mustache. 'Daring Dick of the Black Gang' had a little twisted mustache like Mephistopheles in 'Faust'."

"Oh dear! And the last piece I saw on the Pictures, the villain was clean shaven! That's no guide at all!"

"Girls, you're breaking the silence rule!" said Mrs. Best, opening the door of Dormitory 2, where the conversation, which had begun in whispers, had risen to a pitch audible on the landing outside. "This doesn't look like scoring again next week, and giving another performance. Why, Nora, the rain's driving through that open window straight on to your bed! You'll be getting rheumatism! I shall shut it, and leave the door wide open for air instead. Now be good girls and go to sleep at once. Don't let me hear any more talking."

The Foursomes, in common with most of the hostel, were fond of Mrs. Best, so they turned over obediently, and composed themselves to slumber. They were really tired by this time, and dropped off into the land of Nod before the clock on the stairs had chimed another quarter. How long she slept, Ingred did not know. She dreamt quite a long and circumstantial dream of wandering on the cliffs near the sea with a gentleman-burglar, who was telling her his intention of raiding Buckingham Palace and taking away the Crown Jewels, and she heard his daring designs (as we always do in dreams) without the slightest surprise or any suggestion that the Crown Jewels are kept at the Tower instead of at Buckingham Palace. She woke suddenly, and laughed at the absurdity of the idea.

She felt hot, and threw back her eiderdown. The other girls were sleeping quietly, and the rain was still beating against the window in heavy showers, for it was a stormy night. The door of the bedroom stood wide open. What was that sound coming up the stairs from the hall below? It was certainly not the ticking of the clock. It seemed more like muffled and stealthy footsteps. In an instant Ingred was very wide awake indeed, and listening intently. There it came again! She could not lie still and ignore it. She got out of bed, and with rather shaking knees walked on to the landing and peeped over the banisters. There was a tiny oil-lamp hanging on the wall; it faintly illuminated the stairs. Was that somebody moving about in the darkness of the hall? If it was a burglar, he certainly must not come upstairs, or she would die of fright. An idea occurred to her, and acting on a sudden impulse she dashed into Dormitory 2, roused the others, and told them to snatch what missiles they could, and hurry to her aid.

"We'll fling things at him if he tries to come up!" she gasped, groping for her boots.

It was a horrible experience: four nervous, quaking girls stood in the dim light on the landing gazing down into the haunted blackness of the shadowy hall. The sounds had ceased temporarily, but now they began again - a distinct shuffling as of footsteps, and even a subdued sniff, then the outline of a dark figure made its appearance, bearing straight for the stairs.

With quite commendable bravery Ingred flung her boots at it, which missiles were instantly followed by Nora's hairbrush, Fil's dispatch case, and Verity's pillow. It screamed in a most unburglar-like voice, and apparently with genuine fright.

"If you t-t-t-try to c-c-come nearer, I'll sh-sh-shoot you dead!" quavered Ingred, wishing she had at least some semblance of a pistol to bluff with.

"What *are* you doing, girls?" replied the dark shadow, persisting in its movement towards the staircase, and, as it

Angela Brazil

came into the faint circle of radiance spread by the lamp, resolving itself into the familiar form of Nurse Warner. "Have you suddenly gone mad?"

Here was a situation! The four girls flew back to their dormitoy in great haste, especially as Mrs. Best, disturbed by the noise, had opened her door and come on to the scene in a pink-and-gray dressing gown. They were followed, however, by both Matron and Nurse, and force to give an explanation of their extraordinary conduct.

"I couldn't sleep for the wind, so I put on my felt slippers and my cloak, and went downstairs for a biscuit," declared Nurse Warner, whose voice sounded rather aggrieved. "I didn't think I should disturb anybody."

"You girls are the limit with your silly notions!" said Mrs. Best, really angry for once. "If you fill your heads with absurd ideas about burglars before you go to sleep, of course you can imagine anything. If I hear any more talking in No. 2 another night after the lights are out, I shall separate you, and send each of you to sleep in another dormitory. I'll not have the house upset like this! So you know what to expect. Are you all in your beds? Then not another word!"

"It's very uncomfy without my pillow!" whispered naughty Verity, in distinct disobedience to this mandate, as the door of Mrs. Best's room closed. "Dare I go and fetch it?"

"Sh! Sh! No!"

"I know what we'll give Nursie for a Christmas present," murmured Fil softly. "A nice ornamental tin box of biscuits to keep in her bedroom. She shan't get hungry in the night again, poor dear!"

"*Sh! Sh! Will* you go to sleep!" warned Ingred emphatically.

# CHAPTER X

## THE WHISPERING STONES

The Saxon family had squeezed themselves and certain of their possessions into the little home at Wynch-on-the-Wold, and while flowers still bloomed in the garden and apples hung ripe on the trees it seemed a kind of continuation of their summer holiday; but as the novelty wore off, and stormy weather came on, their altered circumstances began to be more evident. Most of us can make a plucky fight against fate at first - there had been something rather romantic about retiring to the bungalow - but the plain prose of the proceeding was yet to come, and there were certainly many disadvantages to be faced. Mr. Saxon was worried about business affairs; he was a proud, sensitive man, and felt it a great "come down" to be obliged to resign Rotherwood, and the social position it had stood for, and confess himself to the world as one of the "newly poor." It was humiliating to have to walk or take a tram where he had formerly used his car in fulfilling his professional engagements, hard not to be able to entertain his friends, and perhaps hardest of all to be obliged to refuse subscriptions to the numerous charities in the town where his name had always stood conspicuously upon the liberal list. His temper, never his strongest point, suffered under the test, and he would come home from Grovebury in the evenings tired out, moody and fretful, and inclined to find fault with everything and everybody.

It took all his wife's sunny sweetness of disposition to keep the

Angela Brazil

home atmosphere cheerful and peaceful, for Egbert also had a temper, and was bitterly disappointed at not being sent to Cambridge, and at having to settle down in the family office instead. Father and son did not get on remarkably well together. Mr. Saxon, like many parents, pooh-poohed his boy's business efforts, and would sometimes - to Egbert's huge indignation - point out his mistakes before the clerks. He would declare, in a high and mighty way, that his own son should not receive special preference at the office, and so overdid his attitude of impartiality that he contrived to give him a worse time than any of his other articled pupils.

Athelstane, who had begun his medical course at the University of Birkshaw, also had his troubles. He had hoped to study at Guy's Hospital in preparation for the London M.D., and to an ambitious young fellow it was hard to be satisfied with a provincial degree. The thirty-mile motor ride to and from Birkshaw soon lost its charm, and the difficulties of home study in the evenings were great in a bungalow with thin partition walls and a family not always disposed to quiet. As a rule, he kept his feelings to himself, but he went about with a depressed look, and got into a habit of lifting his eyebrows which was leaving permanent lines on a hitherto smooth and unwrinkled forehead.

Pretty Quenrede, who had just left school, was going through the awkward phase of discovering her individuality. At the College, with a full program of lessons and games, she had followed the general lead of the form. Now, cast upon her own resources, she was quite vague as to any special bent or taste. The war-time occupations which had tempted her imagination were no longer available, and *Careers for Women* did not attract her, even if family funds had run to the necessary training. So, for the present, she stayed at home, going once a week to the School of Art at Grovebury, and practicing singing in a rather desultory fashion. Though she pretended to be glad she was an emancipated young lady, as a matter of fact she missed school immensely, and was finding life decidedly slow and tame.

With their elders palpably dissatisfied, Ingred and Hereward would have been hardly human if they had not raised some personal grievances of their own to grumble at, and matters would often have been dismal enough at the bungalow but for Mrs. Saxon's happy capacity for looking on the bright side of things. The whole household centered round "Mother." She was a woman in a thousand. Naturally it had hurt her to relinquish Rotherwood, and it grieved her - for the girls' sake - that most of her old acquaintances in Grovebury had not troubled to pay calls at Wynchcote. The small rooms, the one maid from the Orphanage, the necessity of doing much of the housework herself, the difficulties of shopping on a limited purse, and her husband's fretfulness and fault-finding, might have soured a less unselfish disposition: she had married, however, "for better or for worse," and took the altered circumstances with cheery optimism. She was a great lover of nature and of scenery, and the nearness of the moors, with their ever-changing effects of storm and sunshine, and the opportunities they gave for the study of birds and insects, proved compensation for some of the things which life otherwise lacked.

Every morning, after the fuss of getting off the family to their several avocations, she would run down the garden, and stand for a few minutes by the wall that overlooked the moor, watching great shafts of sunlight fall from a gray sky on to brown wastes of heather and bracken, listening to the call of the curlews or to the trilling autumn warble of the robin, perched on the red-berried hawthorn bush. Kind Mother Nature could always soothe her spirits, and send her back with fresh courage for the day's work. And, in the evening, when husband and children came home to fire and lamp-light, she had generally some nature notes to tell them, or some amusing little incident to make them laugh and forget their various woes and worries.

"I'm so glad, Muvvie dear, you're not a melancholy lugubrious person!" said Ingred once. "It would be *so* trying if you sat at the tea-table and sighed."

"Humor is the salt of life," smiled Mrs. Saxon. "We may just as well get all the fun out of the little daily happenings. Even 'the orphan' has her bright side!"

As "the orphan" was a temporary member of the Wynchcote establishment she merits a word of description. She came from an institution in the neighborhood, and, being the only servant procurable at the time, was tolerated in spite of a terrible propensity for smashing plates, and for carolling at the very pitch of a nasal voice. She was a rough, good-tempered girl, devoted to Minx, the cat, and really kind if anybody had a headache or toothache, but quite without any sense of discrimination: she would show a traveling hawker into the drawing-room, and leave the clergyman standing on the doorstep, took the best serviettes to wipe the china, scoured the silver with Monkey Brand Soap, and systematically bespattered the kitchen tablecloth with ink. Her love of music was a terrible trial to the medical student of the family on Saturday morning, when he was endeavoring to read at home.

"Carlyle says somewhere: 'Give, oh, give me a man who sings at his work!'" growled Athelstane one day, bursting forth from his den to complain of the nuisance, "but I bet the old buffer didn't write that sentiment with a maid-servant howling popular songs in the next room. According to all accounts he loathed noise and couldn't even stand the crowing of a cock. I should call that bit of eloquence just bunkum. If the orphan doesn't stop this voice-production business I shall have to go and slay her. How *can* a fellow study in the midst of such a racket? Where's the Mater? Down in Grovebury? I suppose that accounts for it. While the cat's away, &c."

"Hardly complimentary to compare your maternal relative to a cat!" chuckled Ingred. "Stop the orphan if you can, but you might as well try to stop the brook! She's quiet for five minutes then bursts out into song again like a chirruping cricket or a croaking corn-crake. I want to spiflicate her myself sometimes."

"'Late last night I slew my wife,
   Stretched her on the parquet flooring;
I was loath to take her life,
   But I *had* to stop her snoring!'"

quoted Hereward from *Ruthless Rhymes*.

"Look here!" said Quenrede, emerging from the kitchen with a half-packed lunch basket. "We three are taking sandwiches, and going for a good old tramp over the moors. Why not drop your work for once and come with us? You look as if you needed a holiday."

"I've a beast of a headache," admitted Athelstane.

"You want fresh air, not study," decreed Quenrede with sisterly firmness, "and I shall just make some extra sandwiches and put another apple in the basket. With mother out, the orphan will carol all the morning, unless you gag her, so you may as well accept the inevitable."

"Cut and run, in fact!" added Hereward.

"The voice of the siren tempts me to go - to escape the voice of the siren who stays!" wavered Athelstane.

"Oh, come along, old sport!" urged Ingred. "What are a few old bones to Red Ridge Barrow? You can swat to-night to make up, if you want to."

"It's three to one!" said Athelstane, giving way gracefully; "and there mayn't be any more fine Saturdays for walks."

The four young people started forth with the delightful sense of having the day before them. It was fairly early, and a hazy November sun had not yet drawn the moisture from the heather. On the moor the few trees were bare, but the golden autumn leaves still clothed the woods in the sheltered valley that stretched below. Masses of gossamer covered with dew-drops lay among the bracken, like fairies' washing hung out to dry. There was a hint of hoarfrost under the bushes. The air had that delicious invigorating quality when every breath sets the body dancing. It was too late in the year for flowers, though here and there a little gorse lingered, or a few buttercups and hawkweeds. After about an hour of red haziness the sun pierced the bank of mist and shone out gloriously, almost as in summer; the birds, ready to snatch a moment's joy, were flitting about tweeting and calling, a water-wagtail took a bath in a shallow pool of a stream, and a great flock of bramblings, rare visitors in those parts, paused in their migration to hold a chattering conference round an old elder tree.

The Saxons were determined to-day to go farther afield than their walks had hitherto taken them. The local guide-book mentioned some prehistoric menhirs and a chambered barrow on the top of Red Ridge, a distant hill, so they had fixed that as their Mecca.

It was a considerable tramp, but the bracing air helped them on, and they sat down at last to eat their lunch by the side of the path that led to the summit. The boys had wished to mount to the top without calling a halt, but the girls had struck, and insisted on a rest before the final climb.

"Pity Mother isn't here!" said Ingred, voicing the general feeling of the family, which always missed its central pivot.

"Yes, but it would have been too great a trapse for her, poor darling!" qualified Quenrede. "I don't see how we could get her all this way unless we hired a pony."

"Or borrowed an aeroplane. One seems about as possible as the other," grunted Ingred.

"She shall have a photo of the stones at any rate," said Hereward, fingering his camera. "Hurry up and finish, you girls, or the light will be gone!"

"Well, we can't bolt our sandwiches at the rate you do! I wonder you don't choke!"

The old gray stones stood in a circle on the top of the hill, from whence they had possibly seen four thousand summers and winters pass by. Whether their original purpose was temple, astronomical observatory, or both is one of the riddles of antiquarian research, for neolithic man left no record of his doings beyond the weapons buried with him in his barrow. Legend, however, like a busy gossip, had stepped in and supplied points upon which history was silent. Traditions of the neighborhood explained the menhirs as twelve giants turned into stone by the magic powers of good King Arthur, who, in defiance of the claims of the isle of Avalon, was supposed to be buried in a hitherto unexplored chamber of the large green mound that stood near. Sometimes, so the story ran, the giants whispered to one another, and any one who came there alone at daybreak on May morning might glean much useful information regarding the personal appearance of his or her future lover. As it was obviously difficult to reach so out-of-the-way a spot at such a very early hour, the oracles were seldom consulted at the one and only moment when they were supposed to whisper. There were reputed, however, to be other and easier means of gleaning knowledge from them. Ingred, who had been priming herself with local lore, confided details of the occult ceremonial to Quenrede.

"It sounds rather thrillsome!" admitted that damsel doubtfully. "I'd really like to try it, only the boys would tease me to death. You know what they are!"

"They're going over there to photograph the cromlech. You'd have time before they come back."

"Shall I?"

"Go on!"

"Tell me again what to do."

"You let your hair down, and walk bareheaded in and out and in and out round all the circle of stones. Then you put an offering of flowers on that biggest stone - the Giant King, he's called - and throw a pebble into the little pool below. You count the bubbles that come up - one for A, two for B, &c., - and they'll give you the initial of your future lover. With *very* great luck, you might see his shadow in the pool, but that does not often happen."

"I don't believe in it, of course, but I'll try for fun! The Giant King won't get much in the way of a bouquet to-day!"

Quenrede, protesting her scepticism, but all the same palpably enjoying the magic experiment, picked an indifferent nosegay of the few buttercups, hawkweeds, and late pieces of scabious which were the only flowers available. Then she removed her hair-pins, and, letting down a shower of flaxen hair, commenced her winding pilgrimage among the old gray stones. There is a vein of superstition in the most modern of minds, and she was probably following a custom that had come down the ages from the days when our primitive ancestresses clothed themselves in skins and twisted their prehistoric locks with pins of mammoth ivory. In and out and in and out, with Ingred, like an attendant priestess, behind her, she performed the necessary itinerary, and laid her floral offering upon what may have been the remains of a neolithic altar. The pool below was dark and boggy and brown with peat. She took a good-sized pebble, and flung it into the middle with a terrific splash. Ingred, giggling nervously, counted the bubbles.

"A, B, C, D, E, F, G, H, I - It's 'I,' Queenie! No, there's another! It's 'J'! It's going to be 'J,' old sport! Aren't you thrilled? Oh, I say! Whoever on earth is that?"

Following the direction of her sister's eyes, Quenrede looked through a veil of wind-blown hair, to see, standing among the stones, a stranger of the opposite sex, garbed in tweed knickers and leather gaiters. One glance was enough. The next second she turned, and beat a hurried and ignominious retreat to the sheltered side of the green mound. Ingred, panting in the rear, followed her to cover.

Quenrede, very pink in the face, sat down on a clump of heather and immediately began to put up her hair.

"I never felt such an idiot in my life!" she confided with energy to her sympathetic audience of one. "Ingred! That man knew what I was doing! I saw the horrid amusement in his face. He was laughing at me for all he was worth. I *know* he was!"

At eighteen it is an overwhelming matter to be laughed at. Quenrede's newly-developed dignity was decidedly wounded.

"After all, it was a very schoolgirlish thing to do," she remarked, sticking in hair-pins as well as she could without a mirror. "Do you think he's still there? I shall stop here till he marches off."

"I'll go and prospect," said Ingred.

She came back with the bad news that not only was the stranger still there, but he was actually in close and apparently familiar conversation with Athelstane and Hereward, who were calling loudly for their sisters, and to confirm her words came distant jodellings of:

"Ingred!"

"Queenie!"

"Where are you girls?"

There was nothing for it but to come forth from their retreat. It was impossible to stay hidden forever. Quenrede issued as nonchalantly as she could, with her hair tucked under her tam-o'-shanter, and her gloves on. She bowed instead of shaking hands when Athelstane introduced Mr. Broughten, a fellow-student of his college; it seemed a more grown-up and superior attitude to adopt. She thought his eyes twinkled, but she preserved such an air of stand-off dignity that he promptly suppressed any undue inclinations towards mirth, and stood looking the epitome of grave politeness.

"Broughten knows all about the old barrow," Athelstane explained. "He's got a candle with him - we were duds not to bring one ourselves - and he's going to act showman. Come along!"

The entrance into the mound was through a low doorway with lintel and posts of unhewn stone. Inside was a kind of central hall with three rudely-constructed chambers leading out of it. A pile of rough stones in front seemed to point to further chambers.

"That part's never been explored yet," said Mr. Broughten. "Some of us want to tackle it some day, if we can get permission, but it's a big job. You don't want to bring the barrow down on your head, and be buried in the ruins! I never think the roof looks too secure," he added easily, poking at the stones above with his stick.

The girls, aghast at the notion of a possible subsidence, made a hasty exit to the open air, and hovered near the entrance in much agitation of mind till the rest of the party made a safe reappearance. Their conductor, with a side glance at the bunch of flowers - which Quenrede ignored - made some reference to the Giant King stone and his whispering companions: he was evidently well versed in all old traditions, though he refrained from mentioning local practices. He walked part of the way home with the Saxons before he branched off to the place where he had left his bicycle.

"You look *nice* - you do, *really*, with your hair down," said Ingred to Quenrede that night, as the latter sat wielding her hairbrush at bedtime. "And you needn't be afraid anybody would mistake you for a flapper. Why, Harry Scampton actually asked Hereward the other day if you were married! By the by," she added wickedly, "do you know I've ascertained that Mr. Broughten's Christian name begins with 'J.' Whether 'John' or 'James' I can't say!"

"I don't care if it's Jehosaphat!" snorted Queenie. "I've told you already he doesn't interest me in the least!"

# CHAPTER XI

## ON STRIKE

It was about this time that a general spirit of trouble and dissatisfaction seemed to creep into the school. How and where it started nobody knew, any more than one can trace the origin of influenza germs. There is no epidemic more catching than grumbling, however, and the complaint spread rapidly. It had the unfortunate effect of reacting upon itself. The fact that the girls were restive made the teachers more strict, and that in its turn produced fresh complaints. Miss Burd, careful for the cause of discipline, made a new rule that any form showing a record of a single cross for conduct would be debarred for a week from the use of the asphalt tennis-courts, a decidedly drastic measure, but one that in her opinion was necessary to meet the emergency.

Though the disorder was mostly among the juniors, Va was not altogether immune from the microbe. It really began with a quarrel between Ingred and Beatrice Jackson. The latter was a type of girl common enough in all large schools. She was not always scrupulously honorable over her work, but she liked to curry favor with the mistresses. She copied her exercises shamelessly, would surreptitiously look up words in the midst of unseen Latin translation, and was capable not only of other meannesses, but sometimes of a downright deliberate fib. She and Ingred were at such opposite poles that they did not harmonize well together. In the old days, with visions of parties at Rotherwood, Beatrice had at least been civil, but now that there seemed no further prospect of being asked to pleasant entertainments, she had turned round and treated Ingred with scant politeness in general, and sometimes with deliberate rudeness. Little things that perhaps we laugh at afterwards, hurt very much at the time, and Ingred was passing through an ultra sensitive phase. During the latter part of that autumn term she detested Beatrice.

One day Miss Burd announced that on the following Saturday there was to be a match played in a suburb of Grovebury between two first-class ladies' hockey clubs. She suggested that it might be of advantage to some of the girls to go and watch it, and proposed that each of the upper forms should elect one of their number as special reporter to write an account of the match which could be read aloud afterwards in school. The idea rather struck them.

"It's Finbury Wanderers *versus* Hilton," said Linda Slater, "and they're both jolly good, I know. Wish I could have gone myself, but I'm booked already for Saturday."

"Heaps of us are," said Cicely Denham.

"We'd like to hear about it, though," added Kitty Saunders. "I call it rather a brain wave to choose a reporter."

"Hands up any girls who are free on Saturday!" called Beatrice Jackson.

The announcement had been made rather late, so most of the form already had engagements for the holiday. Only six hands were raised, belonging respectively to Ingred Saxon, Avie Irving, Avis Marlowe, Francie Hall, Bess Haselford, and Beatrice Jackson herself.

"A poor muster for Va!" remarked Kitty. "As Ingred's our warden, I should think she'd better write the report."

"The Finbury ground is a horribly awkward place to get to,"

put in Beatrice. "I suppose you'll motor there, Ingred."

"We have no car now," confessed Ingred, turning very red, for she was sure that Beatrice knew that fact only too well, and had brought it into prominence on purpose to humiliate her.

"Oh! I suppose you'll be motoring, Bess? Couldn't you give some of us a lift?"

"I believe I could take you all," replied Bess pleasantly. "Of course I shall have to ask Dad first if I may have the car out on Saturday, but I don't expect he'll say no."

"Oh, what sport! We'll come, you bet. Look here, I beg to propose that Bess Haselford writes the report of the match."

"And I second it," declared Francie. "Hands up, girls! Bess shall be 'boss' for this show."

Half the girls in the room had not heard Kitty's proposal that Ingred should be chosen, and some of the others, listening imperfectly, had gathered that she was not able to go to the match, so without giving her a further thought they raised hands in favor of Bess, and the matter was carried.

"But indeed I'm no good at writing or describing things!" protested Bess.

"Yes, you are! You've got to try, so there!" cried her friends triumphantly. "You'll do it just as well as anybody else would."

Ingred turned away with a red-hot spot raging under her blouse. That she, the warden of the form, should have been passed over in favor of a girl whose sole qualification seemed to be that she could offer some of the others a lift in her car, was a very nasty knock. Was Bess to supplant her in everything?

"Perhaps you'd like to make her warden instead of me!" she remarked bitterly to Belle Charlton, who stood near. "I'm perfectly willing to resign if you're tired of me!"

Belle only giggled and poked Joanna Powers, who said:

"Don't be nasty, Ingred! Bess is a sport, and we most of us like her."

"I can't see the attraction myself!" snapped Ingred.

She did not want to go to the hockey match now, and made up her mind obstinately that nothing in this wide world should decoy her to it. Bess came to school next morning armed with full permission to use her father's car and to invite as many of her schoolfellows as it would accommodate. She cordially pressed Ingred to join the party.

"I'm not going to the match, thanks," replied the latter frigidly.

"But there's heaps of room - there is indeed, without a frightful squash."

"There's something I want to do at home on Saturday."

"Couldn't you do it in the morning? The form will be disappointed if you don't go - and, I say -" (shyly) "I wish you'd write that wretched report instead of me. I hate the idea of doing it!"

"The form won't care twopence whether I go or stay away, and as they've chosen you to write the report you'll have to write it or it'll be left undone," retorted Ingred perversely.

Bess, looking decidedly hurt, turned away. Her little efforts at friendship with Ingred were invariably met in this most ungracious fashion. She could not understand why her kindly-meant advances should always be so systematically repulsed. Ingred, on her part, stalked off with the mean feeling of one who at bottom knows she is in the wrong, but won't acknowledge it even to herself. Under the sub-current of indignation she realized that she would have liked Bess immensely if only the latter had not taken up her residence at Rotherwood. That, however, was an offense which she deemed it quite impossible ever to forgive.

Ingred went about her work that morning in a very scratchy mood, so much so as to attract the attention of Miss Strong, who possibly felt a little prickly herself, since even teachers have their phases of temper. It was at that time a fashion in the form for the girls to keep all sorts of absurd mascots inside their desks, the collecting and comparison of which afforded them huge satisfaction. Now Miss Strong happened to be lecturing on "The Age of Elizabeth," a subject so congenial to her that she was generally most interesting. But to-day she had reached a rather dry and arid portion of that famous reign, and even her powers of description failed for once and the lesson became a mere catalogue of events and dates. Ingred, bored stiff with listening, secretly opened her desk, and, taking a selection of treasures from it, began to fondle them surreptitiously upon her lap. It was, of course, a quite illegal thing to do. She glanced at them occasionally, but for the most part kept her eyes upon her teacher. Beatrice, however, who sat near and had an excellent view of Ingred's lap, gazed at it with such persistent and marked attention that she attracted the notice of Miss Strong, who followed the direction of her looks and pounced upon the offender.

"Ingred Saxon, what have you there? Bring those things to me immediately and put them on my desk!"

With a crimson face Ingred obeyed, and handed over into the teacher's custody:

1. A black velvet cat.

2. A small golliwog.

3. A piece of four-leaved clover.

4. A stone with a hole in it.

5. An ivory pig.

Miss Strong smiled cynically.

"At fifteen years of age," she remarked, "I should have thought a girl would have advanced a little further than playthings of this description. The Kindergarten would evidently be a more fit form for you than Va! You lose five order marks."

Five order marks! Ingred gasped with amazed indignation. One at a time was the usual forfeit, but to lose five "at one fell swoop" seemed excessive, and would make a considerable difference to her weekly record. She blazed against the injustice. No girl in the form had ever had so severe punishment.

"Oh, Miss Strong!" she protested hotly. "*Five!* I haven't really done anything more than heaps of the others. It's not fair!"

Now if Ingred had really hoped to get her sentence remitted she could not have done a more absolutely suicidal thing. A mistress may overlook some faults, but she will not stand "cheek." The discipline of the form was at stake, and Miss Strong was not a mistress to be trifled with. Her little figure absolutely quivered with dignity, and though physically she was shorter than her pupil, morally she seemed to tower yards. She fixed her clear dark eyes in a kind of hypnotic stare on Ingred and remarked witheringly:

"That will do! I don't allow *any* girl to speak to me in this fashion! You'll take a cross for conduct as well as losing the five order marks. You may go to your seat now."

Ingred walked back to her desk covered with humiliation. To be publicly rebuked before the whole form was an unpleasant experience, particularly for a warden. Beatrice, Francie, and several others were holding up self-righteous noses, though their desks contained an equal assortment of mascots. Ingred, still seething, made little attempt to listen to the rest of the lecture, and was obliged to pass the questions which came to her afterwards on the subject-matter. She was heartily thankful when eleven o'clock brought the brief ten minutes "break."

"Well, you *have* been a lunatic this morning!" said Beatrice, passing her, biscuits in hand, in the cloak-room. "What possessed you to go and lose the tennis-court for the form?"

"If you hadn't stared so hard at me Miss Strong would never have noticed."

"Oh, of course! Throw the blame on somebody else! You're always the 'little white hen that never lays astray.'"

"Kitty and Evie and Belle and I had arranged a set!" grumbled Cicely Denham. "It's most unfair, this rule of punishing the whole form for what one girl does!"

"Go and tell Miss Burd so then!" flared Ingred. "It hasn't been very successful so far to tell teachers they're not fair, but you may have better luck than I had. She'll probably say: 'Oh, yes, Cicely dear, I'll rearrange the rules at once!' So like her, isn't it?"

"Now you're sark! Almost as sarky as the Snark herself!" commented Cicely, as Ingred, choking over a last biscuit, stumped away.

There is much written nowadays about the unconscious power of thought waves, and certainly one grumbler can often spread dissatisfaction through an entire community. Perhaps the black looks which Ingred encountered from the disappointed tennis-players in her form turned into naughty sprites who whispered treason in the ears of the juniors, or perhaps it was a mere coincidence that mutiny suddenly broke out in the Lower School. It began with a company of ten-year-olds who, with pencil boxes and drawing books, were being escorted by Althea

Riley, one of the prefects, along the corridor to the studio. Hitherto, by dint of judicious curbing, they had always walked two and two in decent line and had refrained from prohibited conversation. To-day they surged upstairs in an unseemly rabble, chattering and talking like a flock of rooks or jackdaws at sunset. It was in vain that Althea tried to restore order, her efforts at discipline were simply scouted by the unruly mob, who rushed into the studio helter-skelter, took their places anyhow, and only controlled themselves at the entrance of Miss Godwin, the art mistress.

Althea, flushed, indignant, and most upset, sought her fellow-prefects.

"Shall I go and complain to Miss Burd?" she asked.

"Um - I don't think I should yet," said Lispeth a little doubtfully. "You see, Miss Burd has given us authority and she likes us to use it ourselves as much as we can, without appealing to her. Of course in any extremity she'll support us. I'll pin up a notice in the junior cloak-room and see what effect that has. It may settle them."

Lispeth stayed after four o'clock until the last coat and hat had disappeared from the hooks in the juniors' dressing-room. Then she pinned her ultimatum on their notice board:

"In consequence of the extremely bad behavior of certain girls on the stairs this afternoon, the prefects give notice that should any repetition of such conduct occur, the names of the offenders will be taken and they will be reported to Miss Burd for punishment."

"That ought to finish those kids!" she thought as she pushed in the drawing-pins.

There was more than the usual amount of buzzing conversation next morning as juvenile heads bumped each other in their efforts to read the notice. The result, however,

Angela Brazil

was absolutely unprecedented in the annals of the school. It was the custom of the Sixth Form, and of many of the Fifth, to take their lunch and eat it quietly in the gymnasium. There was no hard and fast rule about this, but it was generally understood to be a privilege of the upper forms only, and intermediates and juniors were not supposed to intrude. To-day most of the elder girls were sitting in clumps at the far end of the gymnasium, when through the open door marched a most amazing procession of juniors. They were headed by Phyllis Smith and Dorrie Barnes carrying between them a small blackboard upon which was chalked:

DOWN WITH PREFECTS!
RIGHTS FOR JUNIORS!
THE WHOLE SCHOOL IS EQUAL!

After these ringleaders marched a determined crowd waving flags made of handkerchiefs fastened to the end of rulers. A band, equipped with combs covered with tissue-paper torn from their drawing-books, played the strains of the "Marseillaise." They advanced towards the seniors in a very truculent fashion.

"Well, really!" exclaimed Lispeth, recovering from her momentary amazement. "What's the meaning of all this, I'd like to know?"

"It's a strike!" said Dorrie proudly, as she and Phyllis paused so as to display the blackboard before the eyes of the Sixth. "We don't see why you big girls should lord it over us any longer. We'll obey the mistresses, but we'll not obey prefects."

"You'll just jolly well do as you're told, you impudent young monkeys!" declared Lispeth, losing her temper. "Here, clear out of this gymnasium at once!"

"We shan't! We've as good a right here as you!"

"We ought to send wardens to the School Parliament."

"We haven't any voice in school affairs!"

"It's not fair!"

"We shan't stand it any longer!"

The shrill voices of the insurgents reached crescendo as they hurled forth their defiance. They were evidently bent on red-hot revolution. Lispeth rose to read the Riot Act.

"If you don't take yourselves off I shall go for Miss Burd, and a nice row you'd get into then. I give you while I count ten. One - two - three - four -"

Whether the strikers would have stood their ground or not is still an unsolved problem, but at that opportune moment the big school bell began to clang, and Miss Willough, the drill mistress, in her blue tunic, entered the gymnasium ready to take her next class. At sight of her, Dorrie hastily wiped the blackboard, and the juniors fled to their own form-rooms, suppressing flags and musical instruments on the way. Miss Willough gazed at them meditatively, but made no comment, and the Sixth, hurrying to a literature lesson, had no time to offer explanations.

Lispeth, more upset than she cared to own, talked the matter over with her mother when she went to dinner at one o'clock. She was a very conscientious girl and anxious to do her duty as "Head." As a result of the home conference she went to Miss Burd, explained the situation, and asked to be allowed to have the whole school together for ten minutes before four o'clock.

"It's only lately there's been this trouble," she said. "I believe if I talk nicely to the girls I can get back my influence. That's what Mother advised. She said 'try persuasion first.'"

"She's right, too," agreed Miss Burd. "If you can get them to obey you willingly it's far better than if I have to step in and put my foot down. What we want is to change the general

Angela Brazil

current of thought."

Speculation was rife in the various forms as the closing bell rang at 3:45 instead of at 4 o'clock, and the girls were told to assemble in the Lecture Hall, and were put on their honor to behave themselves. To their surprise, the mistresses, after seeing them seated, left the room. Miss Burd mounted the platform and announced:

"Lispeth Scott wishes to speak to you all, and I should like you to know that anything she has to say is said with my entire approval and sanction. I hope you will listen to her in perfect silence."

Then she followed the other mistresses.

All eyes were fixed on Lispeth as she ascended the platform. With her tall ample figure, earnest blue eyes, light hair, and fair face flushed with the excitement of her task she looked a typical English girl, and made what she hoped was a typical English speech.

"I asked you to come," she began rather shyly, "because I think lately there have been some misunderstandings in the school, and I want, if possible, to put them straight. There has been a good deal of talk about 'equality,' and some of you say there oughtn't to be prefects. I wonder exactly what you mean by 'equality?' Certainly all girls aren't born with equal talents, yet each separate soul is of value to the community and must not go to waste. The test of a school is not how many show pupils it has turned out, but how *all* its pupils are prepared to face the world. I think we can only do this by sticking together and trying to help each other. In every community, however, there must be leaders. An army would soon go to pieces without its officers! The prefects and wardens have been chosen as leaders, and it ought to be a point of honor with you to uphold their authority. I assure you they don't work for their own good, but for the good of the school. I hear it is a grievance with the juniors that they mayn't elect wardens for the Council. Well -

they shall do that when they're older; it will be something for them to look forward to! There's a privilege, though, that we can and will give them. We're going to start a Junior branch of the Rainbow League, and I think when they're doing their level best to help others, they'll forget about themselves. Carlyle says that the very dullest drudge has the elements of a hero in him if he once sees the chance of aiming at something higher than happiness. Please don't say I'm preaching, for I hate to be a prig! Only we'd all made up our minds to do our 'bit' in 'after the war work,' and it seems such a pity if we forget, and let the tone of the school drop - as it certainly *has* dropped lately. I'm sure if we all think about it we can keep it up, and Seniors and Juniors can work together without any horrid squabbles. We big girls were juniors ourselves once, and you little ones will be seniors some day, so that's one way of looking at it. Now that's all I've got to say, except that any Juniors who like can stay behind now and join the Junior Branch of the Rainbow League. We want to get up a special Scrap-book Union, and Miss Burd says she'll give a prize for the best scrap-book, and also for the best home-made doll. She's going to have an exhibition on breaking-up day."

Angela Brazil

# CHAPTER XII

## THE RAINBOW LEAGUE

Though Lispeth, in her agitation, had not said half the nice things she had intended to say, her little speech had good effect. It reminded the girls of some of the high ideals with which they had started the term, and which, like many high and beautiful things, were in danger of getting crowded out of the way by commoner interests. Everybody suddenly remembered the exhibition and sale which was to come off before Christmas, and made a spurt to send some adequate contribution. The juniors, flattered at having a special branch of their own of the Rainbow League, and time allotted in school to its work, dabbed away blissfully at scrap-book making, with gummy overalls and seccotiny fingers, but complacent faces. The prefects, with intent, dropped in when possible to admire the efforts.

"I believe," said Lispeth to her special confidante Althea, "that perhaps we were making rather a mistake. You can't have any influence with those kids unless you keep well in touch with them. I was so busy, I just let them slide before, and I suppose that was partly why they got out of hand, though the little monkeys had no business to get up that impudent strike! They're as different as possible now, and some of them are quite decent kiddies. Dorrie Barnes brought me a rose this morning. I suppose it was meant as a sort of peace-offering."

It was arranged to hold what was called "The Rainbow Fete"

on breaking-up afternoon, and parents and friends were invited to the ceremony. There was to be both a sale and an exhibition. The best of the toys and little fancy articles were to be at a special stall, and would be sold for the benefit of the "War Orphans' Fund," and those that were not quite up to standard would nevertheless be on view, and would be sent away afterwards to help to deck Christmas trees in the slums. THE stall, as the girls called it, was of course the center of attraction. It was draped with colored muslins in the rainbow tints, and though real irises were unobtainable, some vases of artificial ones formed a very good substitute. The home-made toys were really most creditable to the handicraft-workers, and had been ingeniously contrived with bobbins, small boxes, and slight additions of wood, cardboard, and paper, aided by the color-box. Windmills, whirligigs, carts, engines, trains, dolls' house furniture, jigsaw puzzles, cardboard animals with movable limbs, black velveteen cats with bead eyes, beautifully dressed rag dolls, wool balls and rattles for babies, and dear little books of extracts, were some of the things set out in a tempting display. Fil, whose slim fingers excelled in dainty work, had contributed three charming booklets of poetry and nice bits cut from magazines and newspapers, the back being of colored linen embroidered with devices in silk. They were so pretty that they were all snapped up beforehand, and could have been sold three times over.

"You promised one to me - you know you did!" urged Linda Slater, much aggrieved at the non-performance of an order.

"Well, I thought I'd have time to do four, and could only manage three," apologized Fil. "You see, they really take such ages, and Miss Strong was getting raggy about my prep."

"You *might* make me one for my birthday!" begged Evie.

"Certainly not! Those that ask shan't have!"

"Well, couldn't you do some during the Christmas holidays?"

Angela Brazil

"No, I can't and shan't!" snapped Fil. "I'm sick to death of making booklets, and I'm not going to touch one of them during the holidays. You seem to think I've nothing else to do except cut bits out of magazines for your benefit!"

"There! There! Poor old sport! Don't get baity!"

"You shouldn't do them so jolly well, and then you wouldn't get asked!"

*The* stall occupied a position of importance at the end of the lecture hall, and the rest of the exhibits were put round on trestle tables. They were what Ingred described as "a mixed lot." Some of the animals were bulgy in their proportions, or shaky in their cardboard limbs, the wheels of the carts did not quite correspond, the windmills were apt to stick, or the puzzles would not quite fit. In spite of their imperfections, however, they looked attractive, and would, no doubt, give great pleasure to the little people who were to receive them, and who were hardly likely to be very critical of their workmanship.

To make the afternoon more festive, there was to be a tea stall, to which the girls brought contributions of cakes, and music was to be given from the platform, so that the scene might resemble a café chantant. Ingred had been chosen as one of the artistes, and arrayed in her best brown velveteen dress, with a new pale-yellow hair ribbon, she waited about in her usual agonies of stage fright. Learning from Dr. Linton, however improving it might be to her touch, was hardly conducive to self-complacency, and, after having suffered much vituperation for her imperfect rendering of a piece, it was decidedly appalling to have to play it in public, especially with the horrible possibility that at any moment her master might happen to pop in to view the exhibition and arrive in time for her performance.

"I shall have forty fits if I see him in the room, I know I shall!" she confided to Fil. "You've no idea how he scares me. I have my lessons on the study piano generally, and if only he would sit still I shouldn't mind, but he *will* get up and prowl about the room, and swing out his arms when he's explaining things; he only *just* missed knocking over that pretty statuette of Venus the other day. I'm sure if Miss Burd knew how he flourishes about, she wouldn't let him loose among her cherished ornaments!"

"Perhaps he won't turn up to-day!"

"Oh yes! He said he should make a point of buying a toy for his little boy. If I break down suddenly in the midst of my piece, you'll know the reason. I'm shaking now."

"Poor old sport! Don't take it so hard!"

By three o'clock the lecture hall was filled with what Lilias Ashby (who had undertaken to write a report for the school magazine) described as "a distinguished crowd." Fathers indeed were as few and far between as currants in a war pudding, but mothers, aunts, and sisters had responded nobly to the invitations, and were being conducted round by the girls to see their special exhibits.

Mrs. Saxon had been unable to come that afternoon, but Quenrede had turned up, looking very pretty in a plum-colored hat, and giving herself slight airs as of one who is now a finished young lady, and no longer a mere schoolgirl. She chatted, in rather mincing tones, to Miss Burd herself, while Ingred stood by in awe and amazement, and when she bought a cup of tea from Doreen Hayward at the refreshment stall, she murmured: "Oh, thanks *so* much!" with the manner of a patroness, though only six months ago she and Doreen had sat side by side in the Science Lectures. It was a new phase of Quenrede, which, though accepted to some extent at home, had never shown itself before with quite such aggravated symptoms.

Ingred, walking as it were in her shadow, was not sure whether to admire or laugh. It was, of course, something to have such a pretty and decidedly stylish sister; she appreciated the angle at which the plum-colored hat was set, and the self-restraint that made the tiny iced bun last such an enormous time, when a schoolgirl would have finished it in three bites, and have taken another. A grand manner was certainly rather an asset to the family, and Queenie was palpably impressing some of the intermediates, who poked each other to look at her.

"It's my turn to play soon, and I'm just shivering!" whispered Ingred.

"Nonsense, child! Don't be such a little goose!" declared her sister airily. "It's only a school party - there's really nothing to make a fuss about!"

"*Only* a school party!" That seemed to Ingred the absolute limit. Quenrede last term had, in her turn, shivered and trembled when she had been obliged to mount the platform! Could a few short months have indeed effected so magnificent a change of front?

"All the same, it's I who've got to play, not she! It's easy enough to tell somebody else not to mind," thought Ingred, as, in answer to Miss Clough's beckoning finger, she made her way towards the piano to undergo her ordeal.

One point in favor of the recital was that the audience moved about the room and went on buying toys or cups of tea and cakes, and even talking, instead of sitting on rows of seats doing nothing but watching and listening. It was rather comforting to think that the concert was really only like the performance of a band, a soothing accompaniment to conversation. Ingred opened her music with an almost "don't care" feeling. For one delirious moment she felt at her ease, then, alack! her mood suddenly changed. In a last lightning glance towards the audience she noticed among the crowd near the tea-stall the tall thin figure, cadaverous face, and long lank hair of Dr. Linton. The sight instantly wrecked her world of composure. If it had not been for the fact that Miss Clough was standing near, and nodding to her to begin, she would have run away from the platform.

"Oh, the ill luck of it!" she thought. "If I had only played last time, instead of Gertie, I'd have had it over before he came into the room! I know he'll be just listening to every note, and criticizing!"

With a horrid feeling, as if her breath would not come properly, and her head was slightly spinning, and her hands dithering, Ingred began her "Nocturne," trying with a sort of "drowning" effort to keep her mind on the music in front of her, instead of on the music-master at the other end of the room. For sixteen bars she succeeded, then came the hitch. She had rejected the offered services of Doris Grainger, and had elected to turn over her own pages. She now made a hasty dash at the leaf, her trembling hand was not sufficiently agile, the sheet slipped, she grabbed in vain, and the music fluttered on to the floor. The performance came to a dead halt. Doris and Miss Clough rushed to the rescue, but they were put politely aside by a tall figure who stepped on to the platform, and Dr. Linton himself picked up the scattered sheets of the unfortunate "Nocturne." He arranged them together in order, placed them upon the stand, and, addressing his dismayed pupil, said:

"Now, then, begin again, and *I* shall turn over for you. Bring out that *forte* passage properly! Remember there's a pedal on the piano!"

It was like having a lesson in public. Ingred felt too scared to begin, and yet she was too much afraid of her master to refuse, so the bigger fright prevailed, and - as a cat will swim to escape an enemy - she dashed at the "Nocturne." Once restarted, it went magnificently: afterwards, she always declared that Dr. Linton must have hypnotized her, she was sure her unaided efforts could never have rendered it in such style. He behaved as if he were conducting an orchestra, soothing the *piano* passages and spurring her on to *fortissimo* efforts, even humming the melody in his eccentric fashion, quite unmindful of the audience. The enthusiastic applause at the end was so evidently for both master and pupil that he bowed instinctively in response.

Ingred, remembering, now the ordeal was over, that she was nervous, melted from the platform, and left him to receive the laurels. He did a characteristic but very kind act, looked round for his pupil, and then, perceiving that she had beaten a retreat, sat down to the piano himself, and, unasked, gave an encore for her. A solo from Dr. Linton was an unexpected treat, especially as he was in the mood for music, and played with a sort of rapture that carried his listeners into an ethereal world of delicate sounds. Ingred, hidden behind a protecting barrier of schoolfellows, could see all the sylphs dancing and the fairy pipers piping as the crisp notes came tripping from his practised fingers. At the end she came back as from a dream, to realize that she was not in elf-land, but in the College Lecture Hall, and that she was sitting on a form next to Miss Strong, who held on her knee a little red-coated, brown-haired boy with Dr. Linton's unmistakable dark eyes.

In that instant, as the music ceased, Ingred received quite a sudden and new impression of Miss Strong; there was a tender look on the mistress's face, as she held her arm around the child, and she whispered something to him that made the dark eyes dance. He slipped from her lap, and hand in hand they went together towards the toy-stall. It was quite a pretty little scene, one of those tiny glimpses into other people's lives that we catch occasionally when the veil of their reserve is for a moment held aside. Ingred looked after them meditatively.

"Shouldn't have thought the Snark capable of it," she ruminated. "Perhaps she likes boys better than girls. Some people do."

The toy stall, though half depleted of its contents, was still thecenter of attraction. Lispeth and Althea were displaying what were left of its windmills and whirligigs to friends who bought with an eye to Christmas presents. Miss Strong, reckless in the matter of expense, purchased the *chef-d'œuvre* of the whole collection - a wonderful contrivance consisting of two cardboard towers and a courtyard, across which, by means of a tape wound round bobbins, and turned by a handle, walked a miniature procession of wooden soldiers. Little Kenneth Linton received it with open arms.

"Better let me wrap it up in paper," urged Lispeth. "Somebody said just now that it's beginning to snow, and you don't want to have it spoilt before you get it home, do you?"

"N-no," said Kenneth, relinquishing it doubtfully.

"You're a lucky boy," continued Lispeth, as she made up the parcel. "Isn't that a Teddy Bear in your pocket? And a ball too? There, I believe I've used up all the string! What a nuisance! Can anybody get me any from anywhere?"

"I'll find you some in half a jiff," said Dorrie Barnes, whisking off immediately.

Since the formation of the Junior Rainbow League, Dorrie had taken a liking to Lispeth which amounted to absolute infatuation. She followed her like a pink-faced shadow, and was always at her elbow, sometimes at convenient and sometimes at embarrassing moments. She fled now, like a messenger from Olympus, with the fixed determination of procuring string for her goddess from somewhere. It was not an easy task, for string was a scarce commodity; what there was of it had mostly been already used, and what was left was jealously guarded by its proprietresses, who refused to part with it, even on the plea that it was for the head prefect. Dorrie, however, was a young person of spirit and resource, and she did not mean to be done. One of the trestles that supported the secondary exhibits of toys had rather come to grief, and had been patched up temporarily with stout twine. Her sharp eyes had noted this fact, so, going down on her hands and knees, she managed to creep unobserved under the table, cut the twine with her penknife, and unwound it. She was just congratulating herself upon the success of her achievement when the unexpected happened, or, rather, what might have been expected by any one with an ounce of forethought. The damaged trestle, no longer held together, promptly gave way, and the table collapsed, burying a squealing Dorrie amid a shower of toys. She was pulled out, agitated but uninjured, and the scattered exhibits were carried to another table. In the confusion of their transit she managed to secrete the piece of twine, the loss of which had been the cause of the whole upset, and presented it quite innocently to Lispeth, who, not knowing that she was receiving stolen goods, thanked her and tied the parcel. Ingred, who had watched the whole comedy, laughed, but did not give away the secret.

"That child's an imp!" she said to Quenrede. "But she's a very accomplished imp. I'll tell you the joke afterwards, not now! Lispeth little knows where her string comes from, and she's wrapping up that parcel so placidly! Isn't the Snark looking quite pretty this afternoon? Never saw her with such a color! Well, if you're ready, Queenie, we'll go over to the hostel and get my things. We can just catch the four o'clock train, if we're quick. Wait half a sec, though! There goes Dr. Linton with Kenneth. I don't want to walk out under his wing!"

The tall dark figure of the music master was striding through the doorway, carrying his small son, who hugged his toy with one arm, and waved a friendly good-by with the other.

"What possessed you to drop all your music, child?" said Quenrede, rather patronizingly to Ingred. She was still trying to live up to the plum-colored hat. "You played ever so decently afterwards, though - you did, really! Don't tell me again that you're nervous, for it's all rubbish. You looked as if you enjoyed it."

"Enjoyed it!" echoed Ingred. "If you'd gone through the palpitations that I felt this afternoon you'd want to go to a specialist, and consult him for heart trouble! I've lived through it this once, but if I'm ever asked to play again in public, you'd better go to the cemetery beforehand, and choose a picturesque corner for my grave, and buy a weeping willow ready to plant upon it. Yes, and order a headstone too, with the simple words: 'Died of fright.' I mean it! 'Enjoyed it!' indeed! Why, I've never in the whole of my life been in such an absolutely blue funk!"

# CHAPTER XIII

## QUENREDE COMES OUT

The Saxon family celebrated Christmas at the bungalow with mixed feelings. As Ingred said, it was like the curate's egg - parts of it were very nice. It was the first Christmas they had spent all together for many years, and if they could only have forgotten Rotherwood, and their altered circumstances, they would have enjoyed it immensely. Mrs. Saxon, the unfailing sunshine-radiator of the household, tried to ignore the tone of discontent in her husband's voice, the grumpy attitude of Egbert, Quenrede's fit of the blues, and Athelstane's rather martyred pose. She insisted on bundling everybody out for a blow on the moors.

"If we'd been living in Grovebury," she remarked, "we should probably have taken a jaunt to Wynch-on-the-Wold as a special treat. Let us think ourselves lucky in being on the spot and only having to turn out of our own door to be at once in such lovely scenery. It's like having a country holiday at Christmas instead of midsummer - a thing I always hankered after and never got before!"

Certainly winter on the wold held a charm of its own. The great waste of brown moor stretching under the gray sky showed rich patches where yellow grass and rushes edged dark boggy pools, the low-growing stems of sallows and alders were delicate with shades of orange and mauve; here and there a sprig of furze lingered in flower, and black flights of starlings and fieldfares, driven from colder climates in quest of food, swept in long lines across the horizon. The weather was open for the time of year, the wind strong but not too keen, and had it not been for the lowness of the sun in the sky the day might have been autumn instead of December. It was glorious to walk to the top of Wetherstone Heights and see, miles away, the spire of Monkswell Church and the gleam of the distant river, then to hurry back in the gloaming with the rising mists creeping up like advancing specters, and to find the lamps lighted and tea ready in the cheery bungalow. Nobody wanted to quarrel with Yule cake and muffins, and even Mr. Saxon temporarily forgot his worries and relapsed into quite amusing reminiscences of certain adventures in France.

If only our spirits would keep up to the point to which, with much effort, we screw them, all would be well: unfortunately they often have a tiresome knack of descending with a run. When tea was finished and cleared away Mr. Saxon found the presence of his family a hindrance to reading, and at a hint from their mother the younger members of the party took themselves off into the little drawing-room. Here, round a black fire, which, despite Hereward's poking, refused to burn brightly, the grumble-cloud that had been lowering all day burst at last.

"If we'd only got the Rotherwood billiard table there'd be something to do!" groused Egbert gloomily.

"There isn't a corner in this poky hole where a fellow can fiddle with photography," chimed in Athelstane, "even if there was time to do it. When I get back from Birkshaw it's nothing but grind, grind, grind at medical books all the evening."

"Rather have your job than mine, though," said Egbert. "You haven't to sit under the Pater's eye all day long, and have him down on you like a cartload of bricks if you make the slightest slip. I'm the worst off of the whole lot of us!"

"What about me at that odious Grammar School?" asked

Angela Brazil

Hereward, pressinghis claims to the palm of dissatisfaction.

"Or me at the hostel!" urged Ingred, not to be outdone.

"I don't think you, any of you, realize how slow it is just to stop at home!" sighed Quenrede. "There were sixteen dozen things I'd made up my mind to do, and I can't do one of them. It's going to be a hateful New Year for all of us - just a New Year of going without and scraping and saving and economizing - ugh! What a life!"

"Life's mostly what we make it," said Mother, who had quietly joined the circle. "After all, what we think we want doesn't always give the greatest happiness. Suppose each of us tries to let this be the best year we've ever had? Very little in the way of material wealth may come to us, but the other kind of wealth is far better worth working for. I think this hard time gives us the chance to show what we're made of. During the fighting, the lads at the front went steadily through severe privations, and the women at home worked in the same brave, cheery fashion. Now the strain of the war is over, are we going to let all this splendid spirit drop? Suppose we fight our own battles as we fought our country's? Let me feel I've still got a family of soldiers to be proud of."

"You're the Colonel, then, of the new corps," said Egbert, with an affectionate bear-hug to the slight figure that was already making the black fire break into a blaze. "You've pluck enough for the whole clan, little Mother o' mine! You shall sound your slogan and lead the attack on Fate till we get back to Rotherwood! There!"

"I'm aiming at higher things than Rotherwood, darling boy!" said his mother gravely.

"*I* know!" whispered Quenrede, squeezing the dear hand that reached out and clasped her own. "I won't be a selfish beast any more. I won't indeed. Economizing shall be my New Year's cross!"

"If we're going to count up crosses," proclaimed Athelstane humorously, "the orphan's fine voice while I'm studying is mine!"

"But *she* probably counts it her choicest blessing!" exclaimed Ingred.

And then the whole family broke out laughing, and Mother's little lecture ended in fun. It made its impression upon individual members all the same.

The six miles which separated the Saxons from Grovebury seemed to have set up an effectual barrier between them and the old world in which they had moved before. Many people who had been friendly in the Rotherwood days did not trouble to come so far as Wynch-on-the-Wold to pay calls, and the numerous invitations which had formerly been extended to the young folks decreased this Christmas to very few.

First and foremost amongst these scanty festivities came Mrs. Desmond's dance. It was a grown-up affair, and she had sent printed invitations to Egbert, Athelstane and Quenrede. The latter, who only knew the Desmonds slightly and was always overwhelmed in their presence, developed a sudden and acute fit of shyness and implored to be allowed to refuse.

"If it had been the Browns' or Lawrences' I'd have loved it," she urged, "but you know, Mumsie, how Mrs. Desmond absolutely withers me up! I never can say six words when she's there. I'd run five miles to avoid meeting her: you know I would! She's so starchy."

"You see very little of your hostess at a dance. Don't be silly, Queenie!" insisted Mrs. Saxon. "I say you're to go, so there's an end of it."

"I'll go for an evening's martyrdom, then, not for enjoyment!" wailed her daughter dolefully.

Angela Brazil

A first grown-up dance is often a terrible ordeal to a girl of eighteen, and Quenrede, though she had put on a few airs to impress the schoolgirls at the Rainbow League sale, was at bottom woefully bashful. She was still in the stage when her newly-turned-up hair looked as if it were unaccustomed to be coiled round her head; she had a painful habit of blushing, and had not yet acquired that general *savoir faire* which comes to us with the passing of our teens. To be plunged for a whole evening into the society of a succession of strangers seemed to her anything but an exhilarating prospect.

"If I could just dance with our own boys!" she sighed.

"I'd pity you if you did!" declared Ingred, pausing in an effort to make Athelstane's steps more worthy of a ball-room. "Why, half the fun will be your different partners. I only wish I'd your chance and was 'coming out' too!"

"I'm sure you're welcome to go instead of me," proclaimed Quenrede petulantly.

All the same she watched the preparations for the event with considerable girlish interest. Mother, whose ambitions at first had run to a dress from town, regretfully decided that the family finances could only supply a home-made costume, and set to work with fashion book and sewing-machine to act amateur dressmaker, a thrilling experience to unaccustomed fingers, for paper patterns are sometimes difficult to understand, seams do not fit together as they ought, and the bottom hem of a skirt is the most awkward thing in the world to make hang perfectly straight. Quenrede, standing on the table, revolved slowly while Mrs. Saxon and Ingred stuck in pins and debated whether a quarter of an inch here and there should be raised or lowered. Ingred showed far more cleverness in sewing than her sister; her natty fingers could contrive pretty things already in the shape of collars and blouses.

"You'd make an admirable curate's wife!" Quenrede laughingly assured her. "*I* shall have to marry a rich man and get my things from London."

"It will probably be the other way," declared Mother. "Stand still, Queenie, I can't measure properly if you *will* dance about!"

Though she was ready with a joke, as a matter of fact Quenrede was having a severe struggle not to be snappy. For years and years she had planned her "coming out," and she had decided upon a ball at Rotherwood, and an absolute creation of a gown that was to be sent for from Paris. There would have been some eclat then in emerging from the chrysalis stage of the school-room and becoming a butterfly of society. To make her first grown-up appearance at Mrs. Desmond's dance and in a home-made dress seemed not so much a "coming out" as an "oozing out." There are degrees in butterflies, and she feared her appearance would resemble not the gorgeous "Red Admiral" or "Painted Lady," but the "Common White Cabbage." If it had not been for the New Year's resolution, some traces of her disappointment would have leaked out, but she kept the secret bravely to herself. The family indeed knew she was not anxious to go, but set her unwilling attitude down to mere shyness. Her mother never guessed at the real reason.

There was a tremendous robing on the evening of January the ninth, with Mother and Ingred for lady's-maids, and "The Orphan" hovering about, offering to bring pins or hot water on the chance of getting a peep at the proceedings. Mrs. Saxon stepped back, when all was complete, and viewed the result somewhat in the spirit of an artist who has finished a picture. It is an event in a mother's life when her first little girl grows up and becomes a young lady. To-night Quenrede was to be launched on the stream of society. Looked at critically, her appearance was very satisfactory. Though the new dress might not be up to the level of a fashion-plate, it certainly became her, and set off the pretty fair face, white neck, and coils of gleaming flaxen hair.

"Your gloves and shoes and stockings are all right, and you've got a nice handkerchief, and your fan," reviewed Mother, wrapping an evening cloak round her handiwork. "Good-by, my bird! Enjoy yourself, and don't be silly and shy."

"I shall keep awake till you come back!" Ingred assured her.

It was something at any rate to be going with Egbert and Athelstane. Among the stream of strangers there would be at least two home objects upon which she might occasionally cast anchor. The thought of that buoyed her up as the taxi whirled them down hill to Grovebury.

The Desmonds were giving the dance as a coming-out for one of their own daughters, and their house was *en fête*. An awning protected the porch, red cloth carpeted the steps, a marquee filled the lawn, and a stringed band from Birkshaw had been engaged to play the latest dance music.

Quenrede passed calmly enough through the ordeals of leaving her cloak in the dressing-room (where a crowd of girls were prinking, and there was no room for even a glance in the mirror), and the greeting from her host and hostess in the drawing-room. It was in the ball-room afterwards that her agony began. Egbert and Athelstane were whisked away from her to be introduced to other girls, and utter strangers, whose names she seldom caught, were brought to her, took her program, recorded their initials and passed on to book other partners. The few people in the marquee whom she knew were too far away or too occupied to speak to her, so she stood alone, and heartily wished herself at home.

It was better when the dancing began, though her partners scared her horribly. They all made exactly the same remarks about the excellence of the floor, the taste of the decorations, and the beauty of the music, and asked her if she had been to the pantomime, and whether she played golf. Small talk is an art, and though Quenrede had many interests, and in ordinary circumstances could have discussed them, to-night she felt tongue-tied, and let the ball of conversation drop with a "yes" or "no" or "very." Dances with strangers who expected her to talk were bad enough, but the gaps in her program were worse. No doubt Mrs. Desmond tried to look after all her guests, but several gentlemen haddisappointed her at the last minute, and there were not quite partners enough to go round. At a young people's party Quenrede would have cheerily danced with some other girl in like plight, but at this stiff grown-up gathering she dared not suggest such an informality, and remained a wallflower. She caught glimpses occasionally of Egbert and Athelstane, the former apparently enjoying himself, the latter looking as solemn as if he were in church.

"I know the poor boy's counting his steps and trying not to tread on anybody's toes!" thought Quenrede. "Ingred said his partners would have to pull him around somehow."

Supper was a diversion, for she was taken in by quite a nice red-headed boy, a little younger than herself, who, after a manful effort to talk up to her supposed level, thankfully relapsed into details of football-matches. Being a nephew of the house, he proved an adept in attracting the most tempting dishes of fruit or trifle to their particular table, and even basely commandeered other people's crackers for her benefit. She bade him good-by with regret.

"I say, I wish my card wasn't full! I'd have liked a dance with you!" he murmured wistfully as they left the supper-room.

If only she had known people better, and the atmosphere had not seemed so stiff and formal, and she had not been so miserably shy, Quenrede might have enjoyed herself. As it was she began counting the hours. In one of the wallflower gaps of her program she took a stroll into the conservatory. It looked like fairyland with the colored lanterns hanging among the palms and flowers. Somebody else was apparently enjoying the pretty effect - somebody who turned round rather guiltily as if he were caught; then at sight of her smiled in relief.

"I thought you were one of my hostesses come to round me up

to do my duty," he confessed. "I'm a duffer at dancing, so I've taken cover in here. I see you don't remember me, but we've met before - at Red Ridge Barrow. My name's Broughten."

"Why, of course! You had a piece of candle and showed us inside the mound. I ought to have known you again, but - you look so different -"

"In evening dress! So do you; but I recognized you in a minute. Look here" (in sudden compunction), "am I keeping you from a partner?"

"No more than I am keeping you!" twinkled Quenrede, pointing to the empty line on her program. "I'm not dancing this, so I came here to - to enjoy myself."

Her companion laughed in swift comprehension.

"I don't know how other people may find it," he confided, "but hour after hour of this sort of thing gets on my nerves. A tramp over the moor is far more my line of amusement. I was wishing I might go home!"

"So was I!"

"But there's still at least another hour and a half."

"With extras, more!" admitted Quenrede.

He held out his hand for her program. "I'm an idiot at dancing, but would you mind sitting out a few with me?"

"If you won't talk about the floor and the decorations and the band, and ask me whether I've been to the pantomime, or if I like golf!"

"I promise that those topics shall be utterly and absolutely taboo. I'm sick of them myself."

Quenrede's shyness, which was only an outer casing, had suddenly disappeared in the presence of a fellow-victim of social conventions, and conversation came easily, all the more so after being pent-up all the evening. Henry Desmond, wandering into the conservatory presently, remarked to his partner, sotto voce:

"That Saxon girl's chattering sixteen to the dozen now! Couldn't get a word out of her myself!"

When Quenrede, sometime about five o'clock in the morning, tried to creep stealthily to bed without disturbing her sister, Ingred, refreshed by half a night's sleep, sat up wide awake and demanded details.

"Sh! Sh! Mother said we weren't to talk now, and I must tell you everything afterwards. Oh, I got on better than I expected, though most of the people were rather starchy. How did my dress look? Well - *promise* you won't breathe a word to darling Mother - it was just passable, and that's all. Some girls had *lovely* things. I didn't care. The second part of the evening was far nicer than the first, and I enjoyed the dances that I sat out the most. The conservatory was all hung with lanterns. There; I'm dead tired and I want to go to sleep. Good-night, dear!"

"But you've 'come out!'" said Ingred with satisfaction as she subsided under her eiderdown.

"Oh yes, I'm most decidedly 'out,'" murmured Quenrede.

Angela Brazil

# CHAPTER XIV

## THE PEEP-HOLE

The Foursome League met in Dormitory 2 after the holidays with much clattering of tongues. Each wanted to tell her own experience, and they all talked at once. Fil had a new way of doing her hair, and gave the others no peace till they had duly realized and appreciated it. Verity had been bridesmaid to a cousin, and wished to give full details of the wedding; Nora had played hockey in a Scotch team against a Ladies' Club, and had been promised ten minutes in an aeroplane, but the weather had been too stormy for the flight; the disappointment - when she happened to remember it - quite weighed down her spirits.

"If there's one thing on earth - or rather on air - I'd like to be, it's a flying woman!" she told her friends emphatically. "I'm hoping aeroplanes will get a little cheaper some day, and rich people will keep them instead of motor cars. Then I'll go out as an aviatress. It's a new career for women."

"I wouldn't trust myself to *your* tender mercies, thank you!" shuddered Ingred. "You'd soon bring the machine down with a crash, and smash us to smithereens."

"Indeed I shouldn't! I'd go sailing about like a bird!"

And Nora, suiting action to words, stood on her bed fluttering her arms, till Verity wickedly gave her a push behind, and sent her springing with more force than grace to the floor.

"You Jumbo! You make the room shake!" exclaimed Ingred. "If that's how you're going to land you'll dig a hole in the ground like a bomb! Do move out, and let me get to my drawer! You're growing too big for this bedroom!"

"Nobody's looked at my new hair ribbons yet!" interposed Fil's plaintive voice. "See, I've got six! Aren't they beauties! Pale pink, pale blue, Saxe blue, navy for my gym. costume, black for a useful one, and olive green to go with my velveteen Sunday dress. Don't you think they're nice?"

"Ripping!" agreed Nora. "We'll know where to go when we want to borrow.There, don't look so scared, Baby! I've chopped my hair so short I couldn't wear a ribbon if I tried! It would be off in three racks! Stick them back in their box, and don't tempt me! They're not in my line! I'm going in for uniform. *You*'re the sort who wears chiffons and laces and all the rest of it, but you'll see *me* in gilt buttons before I have done, with wings on them, I hope! I may be the first to fly to Mars! Who knows? You shall all have my photo beforehand just in case!"

Everybody at the College, and particularly at the Hostel, agreed that the first few weeks of the new term were trying. After the interval of the holidays, the yoke of homework seemed doubly heavy, and undoubtedly the prep. was stiffer than ever. Only certain hours were set apart for study during the evenings at the hostel, and any girl who could not accomplish her lessons in that time had to finish them as best she could in odd minutes during the day, or even in bed in the mornings if she happened to wake sufficiently early. Fil, who generally succeeded in mastering about half her preparation and no more, railed at fate.

"I'm so unlucky!" she sighed to a sympathetic audience in No. 2. "I knew the first ten lines of my French poetry beautifully, and I could have said them if Mademoiselle had asked me, but of course she didn't. She set me on those wretched irregular verbs, and they always floor me utterly. As for the 'dictee' - I can't spell in English - let alone French! It's not the least use for Mademoiselle to get excited and stamp her foot at me. I shall be glad when I'm old enough to leave school. I never mean to look at a French book again!"

"How about English spelling?" suggested Ingred. "You'll want to write a letter occasionally!"

"I think by that time," said Fil hopefully, "somebody will have invented a typewriter that can spell for itself. You'll just press a knob for each word, you know!"

"There are about 3000 words in common daily use!" laughed Verity. "If you need a knob for each, your typewriter will have to be the size of a church organ. It'll want a room to itself!"

"Oh, but think of the convenience of it! No more hunting in the dictionary!" declared Fil.

To add to the aggravations of the new term the weather was doubtful, and seemed to take a spiteful pleasure in being particularly wet on hockey afternoons. Day after day, disappointed girls would watch the streaming rain and lament the lack of practice. To give them some form of exercise they were assembled in the gymnasium, and held rival displays of Indian clubs, Morris dancing, or even skipping. "The True Blues" excelled at high jumping, "The Pioneers" at certain rigid balancing feats, "The Old Brigade" were great at vaulting, and "The Amazons" and "The Mermaids" performed marvels in the way of Swedish Boom exercises.

Still, everybody agreed that though the contests were fun in their way they were not hockey, and the girls would much have preferred the playing-fields, however wet, to the gymnasium.

The girls in the hostel had the hour between four and five

o'clock at their own disposal. They were not allowed to leave the College bounds, but they might amuse themselves as they pleased in the garden, playground, or gymnasium. In turns, according to the practising list, they had to devote the time to the piano, and a few even began their prep., though this was not greatly encouraged by Miss Burd, who thought a short brain rest advisable. One afternoon Ingred walked along the corridor with a big pile of music in her arms. Just outside the study she met Verity, and saluted her:

"Cheerio, old sport! Here's Dr. Linton left his whole cargo behind him to-day. He rushed off in a hurry and forgot it, and I know he'll be just raging. I'm going to ask Miss Burd if I may run over into the Abbey and leave it on the organ for him. He has a choir practice to-night, so he's sure to find it. Will you come with me? Right-o! We'll both go in and ask 'exeats.'"

The College was erected upon a plot of land which had originally been part of the Abbey grounds. All the old buildings, formerly inhabited by the monks of St. Bidulph's, and by the nuns in the adjoining convent of St. Mary's, had long ago been swept away, and only a few ruined walls marked their sites. The nave of the Abbey, however, had escaped, and was still in use as a parish church, though the beautiful original chancel and transepts had been battered down by Henry the Eighth's Commissioners. It was only a few hundred yards from the school to the Abbey, and Miss Burd readily gave the girls permission to take Dr. Linton's music and leave it for him on the organ. It was the first time either of them had been inside the church when no service was going on, and they looked round curiously. The organ was locked, or Ingred would certainly never have resisted the temptation to put on the fascinating stops and pedals. She tried to lift the lid that hid the keyboards, but with no success.

"He might have left it open!" she sighed.

"But the verger would come fussing up directly you began to play," said Verity.

Angela Brazil

"I don't see the verger anywhere about."

"Why, no more do I, now you mention it."

"Perhaps he's slipped across to his cottage to have his tea!"

"Perhaps. I say, Ingred, what a gorgeous opportunity to explore. Let's look round a little on our own."

There was nobody to forbid, so they started on a tour of inspection. The places they wanted to look at were those that ordinary church-goers never have a chance of seeing. They peeped into the choir vestry, and Verity gave rather a gasp at the sight of an array of white surplices hanging on the wall like a row of ghosts. They went down a narrow flight of damp steps into a dark place where the coke was kept, they peered into a dusty recess behind the organ, and into a room under the tower, where spare chairs were stored. All this was immensely interesting, but did not quite content them. Verity's ambition soared farther. Very high up on the wall, above the glorious pillars, and just under the clerestory windows, was a narrow passage called the Nuns' Ambulatory. It had been built in the long-ago ages to provide exercise for the sisters in the adjoining convent, to which a covered way had originally led.

"Just think of the poor dears parading round there on wet days when they couldn't walk in their own garden!" said Verity, turning her head almost upside down in her efforts to scan the passage. "I wonder if they ever felt giddy."

"There's a balustrade, of course, but I prefer our modern gym. I believe there's a walk all over the roof too. Athelstane went up once. He said it was like being on the top of a mountain, and you could look all over the town."

"What's that queer stone box thing on the wall?" asked Verity, still gazing upwards.

Ingred followed the line of her friend's eye to a point above the pillars but below the Nuns' Ambulatory. Here, built out like an oriel window, was a curious closed-in-gallery of stone, pierced in places by tiny frets. It seemed to have nothing to do with the architecture of the Abbey, and indeed to be a sort of excrescence which had been added to it at some later date. It spoilt the beauty of line, and would have been better removed.

"Oh, that's the peep-hole!" said Ingred, lowering her head, for it was painful to stretch her neck in so uncomfortable a position. "It was put up in the seventeenth century, when the whole place was full of those old-fashioned high pews. People were very dishonest in those days, and thieves used to come to church on purpose to pick pockets. So they always used to keep somebody stationed up there, looking down through the holes over the congregation to see that no purses were taken during the service. Nice state of things, wasn't it?"

"Rather! But I'd love to go up there. I say, the verger's still at his tea. Shall we try?"

"Right-o! I'm game if you are!"

By the north porch there was a small oak door studded with nails. Generally this was kept locked, but to-day, by a miracle of good fortune, it happened to be open. It was, of course, a very unorthodox thing for the verger to go away and leave the Abbey unattended, even for half an hour, but vergers, after all, are only human, and enjoy a cup of tea as much as other people who do not wear black cassocks. He was safely seated by the fireside in his ivy-colored cottage at the other side of the churchyard, so the girls seized their golden opportunity. They went up and up and up, along a winding staircase for an interminable way. It was dark, and the steps were worn with the tread of seven centuries, and here and there was a broken bit over which they had to clamber with care. At last, after what seemed like mounting the Tower of Babel, they stumbled up through a narrow doorway into the most extraordinary place in the world. They were in the garret of the roof over the

Angela Brazil

south aisle. Above them were enormous beams or rafters, and below, a rough flooring. It was very dim and dusky, but about midway shone a bright shaft of light evidently from some communication with the interior of the nave. Towards this they directed their steps. It was a difficult progress owing to the huge rafters that supported the roof. A plank pathway about four feet above the floor had been laid across the beams, and along this Ingred decided to venture.

She started, balancing herself with her arms, and kept her equilibrium, though the plank was narrow and sprang as she walked. Verity, who had no head for such achievements, preferred to scramble along the floor, creeping under the rafters, in spite of the thick dust of years that lay there. Eventually they both reached the radius of light, and found another doorway leading down by a few steps into what was apparently a cupboard. In the wall of the cupboard, however, were frets through which the sunlight was streaming. Ingred applied an eye and gave a gasp of satisfaction.

They were in the peep-hole on the wall of the nave, and could gaze straight down into the church below. It was marvellous what an excellent view they obtained. Nothing was hidden, not even the interiors of the old-fashioned square pews that had lingered as a relic of the eighteenth century. Anybody stationed in this spy-box would certainly be able to keep guard over the congregation, and note any nefarious designs on the pockets of the worshipers.

For the moment the church was empty, then footsteps were audible in the porch. Was it the verger returning from his tea? The girls began to flutter at the prospect of his wrath if he discovered them. It was no cassock-clad verger that entered, however, but two young people, far too much interested in each other to gaze upwards towards the frets of the peep-hole. They thought they had the church to themselves, and walked along conversing in a low tone. The particular shade of flaxen hair in the masculine figure seemed familiar, and Ingred chuckled as she recognized her eldest brother.

"Caught you, old boy! Caught you neatly!" she thought. "Who's the girl? Oh, I know. It's one of the Bertrands - Queenie said they were at the Desmonds' dance, so I suppose he met her there. What a priceless joke! How I shall crow over him for this! They're actually going to sit down in a pew and talk! Well, this is the limit!"

Quite unconscious that sisterly eyes were watching, Egbert ushered his fair partner into one of the old-fashioned square pews. It was a quiet place to rest, and perhaps the young lady was tired. He sat by her side, very much occupied in explaining something which the girls in the peep-hole could not overhear. At last the quiet well-trained footsteps of the verger echoed again in the nave. He glanced at the young couple in the pew, and began to dust and rearrange the hymn-books. Egbert and Miss Bertrand took the hint and departed.

The pair spying through the fretwork above also judged it expedient to beat a hasty retreat. They were terrified lest the verger should remember that he had left the tower door open, and should lock them in. They stumbled back among the rafters, regardless of dust, and groped their rather perilous way down the winding staircase. To their infinite relief the door was not shut, and they were able to creep quietly out and bolt from the Abbey unperceived. They fled along the stone path that edged the churchyard, then stopped under the shelter of a ruined wall to brush the dust off their dresses before re-entering the College.

"It's been quite an adventure!" gasped Verity.

"Rather! Particularly catching old Egbert. Won't he look silly when I bring it out before the family? I don't know whether I *will* tell them, though! I think I'll keep it back, so as to have something to hold over his head when he teases me. Yes, that would be far more fun, really. I can hint darkly that I know one of his secrets, and he'll be so puzzled. I don't admire his taste much. Queenie detests those Bertrand girls. I don't know them myself to speak to, but I'm not impressed. Look here, the dust simply *won't* come off your skirt, Verity!"

"It'll do as it is, then, and I'll use the clothes brush afterwards. Don't worry any more. There's the Abbey clock striking five! It's a few minutes fast, fortunately, but we shall simply have to sprint, or we shall be late for tea!"

# CHAPTER XV

## BROTHERLY BREEZES

There was no doubt that Egbert was the odd one in the Saxon family. He had inherited a testy strain of temper, and was frequently most obstinate and perverse. It was unfortunate that he was an articled pupil in his father's office, for he fretted and tried Mr. Saxon far more than Athelstane would have done in the circumstances. Egbert's saving quality was his intense love for his mother. Her influence held him steadily to his work, and smoothed over many difficult situations. He was apt to quarrel with Quenrede, but he had a soft corner for Ingred, and sometimes made rather a pet of her.

A few days after the incident at the Abbey he turned up at school, to her immense astonishment, and asked leave from Miss Burd to take her out to tea at a cafe. It had been an old promise on his part, ever since Ingred went to the hostel, but it had hung fire so long that she had come to regard it as one of those piecrust promises that elder members of a family frequently make, and never find it convenient to carry out. She had reminded Egbert of it at intervals all through the autumn term, then had given it up as "a bad job." To find him waiting for her in Miss Burd's study, ready to escort her to the Alhambra tea-rooms, seemed like a fairy tale come true. She whisked off at once to make the best possible toilet in the circumstances, and reappeared smilingly ready. When you have tea every day at a long table full of girls, the meal is apt to grow monotonous, and it was a welcome change to take it

Angela Brazil

instead in a gay Oriental room with Moorish decorations and luxurious arm-chairs, and a platform in a corner, where musicians were giving a capital concert. Ingred leaned back on an embroidered cushion and ate cakes covered with pink sugar, and listened to a violin solo followed by some charming songs, and watched the gay crowd sitting at the other small tables. It was really delightful to be out just with Egbert alone. It made her feel almost grown-up. Moreover, he was in such a remarkably generous mood. He set no limit to the supply of cakes, and he stopped at the counter as they went downstairs and bought her a box of chocolates and a large packet of Edinburgh rock. He even went further, for as they walked round the square together, and looked into the window of a fancy shop, he told her to choose her birthday present, and agreed amicably when she selected a morocco-leather bag which was for the moment the summit of her dreams. She parted from him at the College gates in deepest gratitude. This was indeed something like a brother!

"You're an absolute trump!" she assured him.

"Well, a fellow's always got a decent sister to take about, anyway," he replied enigmatically, a remark over which Ingred pondered, but could not fathom.

She mentioned the jaunt at the family supper-table on Friday evening. To her immense surprise her innocent remark had somewhat the effect of a bomb. Mr. Saxon turned to his son with a sudden keen expression, as if he had convicted him of a crime. Mrs. Saxon's face also was full of suppressed meaning, while Egbert colored furiously, looked thunderous at his sister, and relapsed into sulky silence. Poor Ingred felt that she had, quite unconsciously, put her foot in it, though how or why she could not tell. She said no more at the time, and when, afterwards, she ventured to refer again to the subject, she was so tremendously shut up that she saw clearly it was discreet to make no further inquiry. Plainly there was some tremendous quarrel between Egbert and his father, for they were barely on speaking terms.

Mr. Saxon threw out occasional inuendoes that caused his son finally to stump from the room. Mrs. Saxon went about with a cloud of distress on her face, and Quenrede, to whom Ingred applied for enlightenment, promptly and pointedly changed the subject. It was miserably uncomfortable, for father and son were like two Leyden jars charged with electricity, and ready to let fly at any moment. It was only the mother's influence that averted a family thunderstorm. Athelstane, too, seemed in the depths of gloom. He was willing, however, to communicate his woes.

"I want a whole heap more medical books," he confided to his sister, "and Dad says he can't get them, and I must manage without. How on earth *can* I manage without. What's the use of my going to College if I haven't the proper textbooks? I can't always be borrowing. If I fail in my exams, it will be his fault, not mine. He's the most absolutely unreasonable man anybody could have to deal with. Of course I know they're expensive, and funds are low, but I've simply *got* to have them, or chuck up medicine!"

"It's so terrible to be poor!" sighed Quenrede, thinking of the old, happy pre-war days at Rotherwood, when everything came so easily, and there were no struggles to make ends meet.

She talked the matter over afterwards with Ingred.

"If I could only help somehow!" she mourned. "I've often thought I might go out and earn something, but Mother's not strong, and I really do a great deal in the house. If I went away and left her with only 'The Orphan,' she'd be laid up in a fortnight. As it is, she tries to do far too much. How could we possibly get some money for Athelstane's books? We'd rather die than ask our friends!"

Ingred shook her head sadly. Wild ideas surged through her mind of disguising herself and sweeping a crossing - there were stories of wealthy crossing-sweepers - or rivaling Charlie Chaplin on the cinema stage, but somehow they did not seem quite practicable for a girl of sixteen. She left Quenrede's question unanswered. It was only late on Saturday afternoon that a great idea came to her. Great - but so overwhelming that she winced at the bare notion. It was as if some inner voice said to her: "Sell Derry!" Now Derry, the fox terrier, was her very own property. He had been given to her two years before by a cousin as a birthday present. He was of prize breed, and had brought his pedigree with him. He was a smart, bright little fellow, and on the whole a favorite in the household, though he sometimes got into trouble for jumping on to the best chairs and leaving his hairs on the cushions. It had never particularly struck Ingred that Derry was of value, until last week, when Mr. Hardcastle noticed him. Relations with that precise old neighbor next door had been rather strained for a long time, since the unfortunate episode when Hereward had unwittingly discharged the contents of the garden syringe in his face. For months he studiously avoided them, calling his collie away with quite unnecessary caution if they happened to pass him on the road, and bolting into his own premises if they met near the gate. But one day, about Christmas-time, Sam, the collie, who was a giddy and irresponsible sort of dog, given to aimless yapping at passing conveyances, overdid his supposed guardianship of his owner's property, and blundered into a motor that was whisking by. The car did not trouble to stop, and when it was a hundred yards away, Sam picked himself up and limped on three legs to show his bleeding paw to his agitated master. Fortunately Athelstane, from the bungalow garden, had witnessed the accident, and came forward like a Good Samaritan with offers of help. His elementary acquaintance with surgery stood him in good stead, and he neatly set the injured limb, and bound it up with splints and plaster. There had been many inquiries over the hedge as to the invalid's progress, and congratulations when the bandages were able at last to be removed. Old Mr. Hardcastle had waxed quite friendly as he expressed his thanks, and one day, catching Ingred by the gate with Derry, he had volunteered the information that "that fox terrier of yours is a fine dog, and no mistake, and would be worth something to a fancier!"

"Sell Derry!" the idea, though she hated it, had taken possession of Ingred's brain. He was the only thing she had that was of marketable value. To part with the poor little fellow would be like selling her birthright, but, after all, brothers came first, and how could Athelstane study without books? Something Mother had said the other day clamored in her memory. "If we've lost our fortune we've got our family intact, and we must stick tight together, and be ready to make sacrifices for one another." Ingred had quite made up her mind. She put on her hat, took Derry from his cozy place by the kitchen fire, kissed his nose, and, carrying him in her arms, walked to the next-door house, rang the bell, and asked to see Mr. Hardcastle.

She found the old gentleman in a cozy dining-room, seated by a cheery fire, and reading the evening paper. He looked a little astonished when she was ushered in, but received her politely, as if it was quite a matter of course for a young lady, hugging a dog, to pay him an afternoon visit.

Ingred put Derry down on the hearth rug, took the arm-chair that was offered her, and with a beating heart and a very high color plunged into business, and inquired if it were possible to find a fancier who wished to buy a prize fox terrier.

"I've his pedigree here," she finished, "and he really is a nice little dog. If you know of anybody, I'd be so glad if you would tell me please!"

Mr. Hardcastle, evidently much electrified, knitted his bushy eyebrows in thought, and pursed his mouth into a button.

"There was a vet. in Grovesbury who told me a while ago that he wanted one, but I saw him yesterday, and he said he had just bought one, so that's no good! You might try the advertisements in *The Bazaar*. He looks a bright little chap. Why are you in such a panic to get rid of him? Been killing chickens?"

"No," said Ingred, turning pinker still; "it isn't that - I don't want to sell him, of course - only - only -"

And then to her extreme annoyance, her brimming eyes overflowed, and she burst into stifled sobs.

The old gentleman shot his lips in and out in mingled consternation and sympathy.

"There! There! There!" he exclaimed. "Don't cry! For goodness' sake, don't cry! Tell me, whatever's the matter?"

It was, of course, a most unorthodox thing for Ingred to blurt out family affairs, and Father and Mother would have been justly indignant had they known, but she was impulsive, and without much worldly wisdom, and Mr. Hardcastle seemed sympathetic, so on the spur of the moment she told him the urgency of Athelstane's need, and how she was trying to meet it. He sat quite quiet for a short time, staring into the fire, then he said, very gently and kindly:

"My dear little girl, you needn't part with your dog. I believe I can lend your brother all the medical books he wants."

"You! But you're not a doctor?" exclaimed Ingred.

"No, but my boy was studying medicine at Birkshaw. He had just passed his intermediate M. B. when he was called up. I've got all his books. He won't want them again now. He was flying over the German lines, and his machine crashed down. One comfort, he was killed instantly! He had always hoped he'd never be taken prisoner. I think he'd have liked his books to be put to some use. I'll hunt them out, and send them across to your brother, and the microscope, and any other things I can find. He may just as well have them."

There was a huskiness in the old gentleman's voice, but he coughed it away.

"I don't know how to thank you!" stammered Ingred.

"I don't want any thanks. It's only a neighborly act. Take your dog home, and say nothing about all this. I'll write to your brother. I wonder I never thought about it before!"

Mr. Hardcastle was as good as his word, for next Monday evening quite a large consignment arrived for Athelstane, with a note offering the loan of books and microscope if they would be of any service in his medical studies.

"Why, they're absolutely the very things I wanted!" exclaimed that youth rapturously. "What a trump he is! A real good sort! I say, you know, it's really most awfully kind of him! I wonder what the Dickens put it into his head?"

But on that point none of the family could enlighten him, for only Ingred and Derry knew the secret, and Ingred was at school, while Derry, belonging to the dumb creation, expressed his opinions solely in barks.

When the household was reunited for next week-end, the clouds had cleared from Athelstane's horizon, but seemed to have settled more darkly than ever round Egbert. There was a horrible feeling of impending storm in the home atmosphere. It lent a constraint to conversation at meals, and put an effectual stopper on the fun which generally circulated round the fireside. It was all the more uncomfortable because nobody voiced the cause.

"Father looks unutterables, Mother's plainly worried to death, Egbert is sulks personified, Queenie won't tell, Athelstane and Hereward either don't know or don't care what's the matter, but it makes them cross. What is one to do with such a family?" thought Ingred on Sunday afternoon.

It had been wet, and, though a detachment of them had ventured to church in waterproofs, they had not been able to take their usual safety valve of a walk across the moors. Seven people in a small house seem to get in one another's way on Sunday afternoons. Father was dozing in the dining-room, Mother, Athelstane and Hereward were in the drawing-room, interrupting each other's reading by constant extracts from their own books; Ingred, who hated to pause in the midst of *The Scarlet Pimpernel* to hear choice bits from *The Young Visiters* or *Parisian Sketches*, sought sanctuary in her bedroom, only to find the blind drawn and Quenrede with a bad headache, trying to rest. There seemed no comfortable corner available, so she slipped on her thick coat, put her book in the pocket, and walked down the garden to sit in the cycle-shed. Even in the rain it was nice out of doors; clumps of purple and yellow crocuses showed under the gooseberry bushes; lilies were pushing up green heads through the soil; the flowering currant was bursting into bud; roots of polyanthus flaunted mauve and orange blossoms; under a sheltered wall were even a few early violets, whose sweet fresh scent seemed as the first breath of spring. A missel-thrush on the bare pear tree sang triumphantly through the rain, and a song-thrush, with more melodious notes, trilled forth an occasional call; the robin, which had haunted the garden all the winter, was scraping energetically for grubs among the ivy on the wall, and scarcely troubled to fly away at her approach.

Ingred drew great breaths of sweet-scented wet air, and, with almost the same instinct as the thrush, broke into "Thank God for a Garden!" the song that Mother loved to hear Quenrede sing in the evenings when the day's work was over.

Delightful and refreshing and soothing as Nature may be, however, it is rather a wet business to stand admiring crocuses in the streaming rain, so Ingred made a dash through the dripping bushes to the cycle-shed. If she had calculated upon finding solitude here she was disappointed. It was occupied already. Egbert, looking as gloomy as Hamlet, was tinkering with the motor-bicycle. He greeted his sister with something between a sigh and a grunt, whistled monotonously for a moment or two, then burst into confidence.

"Look here, Ingred; I can't stand this any longer. I wish I were back in the army! I've a jolly good mind to chuck everything up, and re-enlist!"

"Is it as bad as all that?" asked Ingred.

"Yes, I'm about fed up with life. If it weren't for the little Mater I'd have cleared out before this. Perhaps she'll miss me, but I don't know that anybody else will, and I don't care!"

"How about Miss Bertrand?" asked Ingred, obeying a sudden impulse of mischief.

Egbert flung down a spanner, and turned to her the most astonished face in the world.

"What do *you* know about Miss Bertrand?" he queried.

Ingred chuckled delightedly. To use her own schoolgirl expression, she felt she "had him on toast."

"More than you imagine! Who went into the Abbey Church, I should like to know, and sat in a pew for ever so long, and looked tender nothings? Oh yes! *I* saw you, and a pretty sight it was, too!" she teased.

Egbert was gazing at her as if he could scarcely believe his senses.

"But - but - where were you?" he stuttered.

"In the peep-hole!" exploded Ingred. "I could see right down into the church, and I watched you come in! I've been saving this up!"

Egbert drew a long breath.

"If I'd only known before!" he said slowly. "Ingred, stop laughing! You don't understand. Look here, will you go and tell Dad that you saw me there, and the exact day and time when it happened. You can remember that?"

"Why, surely Father's the very last person you want to know?" said Ingred, sobering down.

"No, he isn't, he's the one it's most important should hear about it from a reliable witness whom he can believe. I don't mind telling you about it now" (as Ingred expressed her astonishment in her face), "I'd got myself into a jolly old mess, and you'll be able to clear me! It was this way; I slipped out from the office one afternoon for an hour, and went into the Abbey as you saw. Well, when I got back, somebody had been into Dad's room during his absence, and a small sum of money was missing. He taxed me with taking it!"

"*You!* But why you?" exclaimed Ingred indignantly.

"Because I was the only person who had access to his private room. I told Dad I had been out - which made him angrier still - but none of the clerks had happened to see me go or come back, and I had no other witness to prove my words. As a matter of fact, I went out before Father, and came back after he had returned, but he wouldn't take my word for it. You know what he is when he's angry. You simply can't argue with him! Then you made things ever so much worse by blurting out how I'd taken you to tea at the cafe, and bought you a bag. Father glared as if it proved I'd been spending stolen money!"

"You were rather flush of cash that day," commented Ingred.

"Yes, the fact is I'd been writing a short story, and it had been accepted by a newspaper. It's a poor enough thing, and I didn't sign my own name to it. I didn't want to tell them at home I was trying to write until I could do something better. Anyhow, I'd just cashed the check, and thought I'd give you a treat for once. I knew it was no use to explain to Father. Mother has stuck up for me, but I can tell you I've been having a time of it this last fortnight."

"But, Egbert," said Ingred, frankly puzzled, "couldn't you have got Miss Bertrand to tell Dad where you were? It would have been better after all than letting him think you took the money."

Egbert's face darkened again tragically.

"I wouldn't appeal to Miss Bertrand to clear my character if it were a charge of murder. I'd be hanged first! I met her the very day after we were in the Abbey together - she was walking with some idiot of an airman - and she stared straight in my face and cut me. I've done with girls! They're all of them alike!" and the gloomy young misanthrope picked up the spanner and began energetically tightening nuts on the motorcycle.

Ingred shook a sympathetic head. She had not much experience in love affairs, but she fancied that this one did not go very deep.

"You'll get over it," she consoled. "And she wasn't a very nice girl, anyway. Queenie always loathed her. If Dad's had his nap, I'll go and tell him how I saw you in the Abbey. I know it was a Tuesday, because I'd had my music lesson, and was taking the books that Dr. Linton left behind him."

"Good! That's what's called proving an alibi. I don't know who walked off with those notes, but as long as Dad's satisfied I had nothing to do with it, that's all I care. He can thrash it out with the clerks now, or leave it alone."

Mr. Saxon questioned Ingred closely, but accepted her account of the matter, which set his doubts at rest concerning his son. The relief in the family circle was enormous. Mother's face was beaming, and it seemed as if the storm-clouds had blown away, and the sun had shone out. Tea was the most comfortable meal that the household had taken together for a fortnight.

"I haven't spent quite all that check I got from the *Harlow Weekly News*," whispered Egbert to Ingred that evening, "and

Angela Brazil

I'm going to buy you a box of chocolates on Monday. I'll leave them for you at the Hostel. You deserve them!"

"You mascot! I can't quite see that I *do* deserve them, for I really meant to rag you about that Abbey business. But I won't say 'No, thank you!' to chocks! Rather not! We'll have a gorgeous little private feast in No. 2 to-morrow night."

# CHAPTER XVI

## AN EASTER PILGRIMAGE

The thirteen weeks between Christmas and Easter dragged much more slowly than those of the autumn term. The weather was cold and variable. As fast as Spring stirred in the earth, Winter seemed to stretch forth chilly fingers to check her advent. Nature, like a careful mother, kept the buds tightly folded on the trees and the yellow daffodil blossoms securely hidden under their green casement curtains. Only the most foolhardy birds ventured to begin building operations. The rooks in the elm trees near the Abbey had begun to repair their nests during a mild spurt in January, then put off further alterations till late in March. Morning after morning the girls would wake to find the roofs covered with hoar frost. Ingred, who hated the cold, shivered as she crossed the windy quadrangle from the college to the hostel, and congratulated herself that she lived in the days of modern comforts.

"How the old monks and nuns managed to exist in those wretched chilly damp cloisters I can't imagine," she said, as she squatted by the stove warming her hands. "Were they allowed to take hot bricks to bed with them in their cells? Think of turning out for midnight services into an unwarmed church! It sounds absolutely miserable!"

"Perhaps they made themselves more comfortable than we think," commented Verity. "One of them probably kept up the fire and doled out hot drinks after the services. It might

Angela Brazil

even have been possible to take a hot-water bottle to church under the folds of those ample habits."

"I don't believe that would have been allowed. Surely the cold was part of the discipline."

"I shouldn't have been a nun if I'd lived in the Middle Ages," said Fil. "I'd have wanted to go to the tournaments and to have seen my knight fighting with my ribbons in his helmet and bringing me the crown. Oh, wouldn't it have been fun? Life's not a scrap romantic nowadays. I do think men are slackers. Why don't they wear their ladies' colors at football, and let whoever gets a goal carry a wreath of flowers to the pavilion and crown his girl 'Queen of Beauty'? There'd be some excitement in looking on then. As it is it's nothing but a scrimmage; and I never care a button which side wins. You needn't laugh. Why shouldn't a footballer look gallant and present trophies? The world would jog on a great deal better if there were more chivalry in it."

"The girls want to play games themselves nowadays instead of looking on and receiving trophies," giggled Verity.

"I don't!" declared Fil emphatically. "I hate tearing about at hockey, or running at cricket. I'd far rather let my knight do the work for me."

"Chilly work looking on in this weather. The games keep one warm," said Ingred, who was still only half thawed.

In spite of boisterous March winds and late spring frosts the sun climbed steadily higher in the sky and the days lengthened. Ingred, who used to arrive home in the twilight at Wynchcote on Friday afternoons, could now dig in the garden after tea. She liked the scent of newly-turned earth, and was happy working away with a trowel transplanting roots of wall-flowers and forget-me-nots to make a display in the bed near the dining-room window. At school the various forms vied with one another in shows of hyacinths grown in bowls, the best of which were lent to the studio on drawing days and figured as models for water-color sketches, together with daffodils and hazel catkins. Lispeth, who did not relax the activities of The Rainbow League, revived her idea of a Posy Union, persuaded some of the girls to bring little pots of gay crocuses or blue squills to school, and after these had been duly exhibited on a table in the lecture-hall, sent them through the agency of a "Children's Welfare Worker" to brighten the bedsides of various small invalids in the poorer quarters of the town and let them know that spring had arrived.

Easter-tide was very near now, and the school would break up for three weeks. Miss Burd was going away to allow her tired brains to lie fallow for a while, and most of the other teachers were looking forward to a well-earned rest apart from their forms. It came as a surprise to everybody when Miss Strong - alone - among the staff - suggested the project of taking some of her pupils for a short walking tour. They were to start off, like pilgrims of old, carrying with them the barest necessaries, and have a four days' tramp to visit a few of the beauty spots of the neighborhood, spending a couple of nights *en route*.

"It will be a real open-air holiday," she assured them. "We shall be out of doors all day long and eat most of our meals by the roadside. I've planned it out carefully. A short railway journey to Carford, then walk by easy stages through Ryton-on-the-Heath to Dropwick and Pursborough, where we can get the train again back to Grovebury. I know of two extremely nice Temperance Hotels where we can be put up for the night. By going in this way we shall see the cream of the country. Any girl who is a good walker may join the party."

It certainly sounded a fascinating program, and after due consideration at home eight girls put their names down for the excursion - Ingred, Verity, Nora, Bess, Linda, Francie, Kitty, and Belle. They felt it would be quite a new experience to know Miss Strong out of school hours; the light in her eyes when she announced the scheme gave promise of hitherto hidden capacities for fun. It circulated round the form that she

Angela Brazil

might prove quite a jolly companion. Those girls who could not join the tour were a trifle wistful and inclined towards envy. They took it out of the pilgrims in gloomy prognostications concerning the weather.

"It will probably rain all the time and you'll tramp along like a row of drowned rats," suggested Beatrice.

"It won't do anything of the sort. I believe we're going to have a fine mild spell and it will be just glorious. I'm taking my 'Brownie,' so there'll be some snapshots to show we've been enjoying ourselves," retorted Nora briskly. "You stay-at-homes will be sorry for yourselves when you hear our adventures!"

To allow the weather ample chance of improvement, and perhaps also to give Miss Strong time to rest, the excursion was fixed for the last week of the holidays. One morning in mid-April, therefore, found teacher and pupils meeting together on the platform of Grovebury station to catch the 9.25 train to Carford. They wore jerseys and their school hats, and they carried their luggage according to their individual ideas of convenience. Linda wore her little brother's satchel slung over her back. Nora had borrowed a knapsack, Kitty preferred a parcel, Verity packed her possessions in a string bag, and Bess carried a neat dispatch-case.

"I'd a ripping idea for mine, but it wouldn't work," declared Ingred. "I meant to tie my parcel to a balloon and then just lead it along by a string. But I couldn't get a proper gas balloon for the business, and that's what you ought to have."

"And suppose the wind were to blow it away from you, what then?" inquired Miss Strong.

"I suppose I should have to cable it round my waist."

"Then you might be whisked up with it, and we should see you sailing off into the clouds in a kind of aeroplane holiday instead of a walking tour! I don't think we can patent your balloon dodge yet."

"What I want," said Kitty, "is a sort of child's light mail-cart arrangement that I could wheel along. It's what Mother always says she needs for shopping - a parcel-holder on wheels. Why doesn't somebody invent one? He - or she (I'm sure it would be a *she*) - would make a fortune."

"We might have borrowed a perambulator," said Belle, quite seriously, "and have packed all our luggage into it."

"Oh, I dare say! And who would have wheeled it?"

"We could have taken it in turns."

"With long turns for the willing horses, and short turns for shirkers! No, thanks! Better each to stick to our own."

"Besides which, forget stiles. We hope to try some field paths as well as high roads," added Miss Strong. "Also I should decidedly have jibbed at escorting a perambulator. Here comes the train! Let us make a dash for an empty carriage and keep it to ourselves."

It was only a short journey to Carford, but it took them over twelve rather uninteresting miles and put them down just at the commencement of a very beautiful stretch of country where open uplands alternated with wooded coombes, and where the stone-roofed villages were the prettiest in the county.

Miss Strong, who had had some experience of mountaineering in Switzerland, restrained the pace and kept them all at what she called a "guide's walk."

"It pays in the long run," she assured them. "If you tear ahead at first, you get tired later on, and we must keep fairly well together. I can't have some of you half a mile behind."

The April days were still cold, but very bracing for exercise. Lambs were out in the fields, primroses grew in clumps under the hedgerows, hazel catkins flung showers of pollen to the winds, and in the coppice that bordered the road pale-mauve March violets and white anemone stars showed through last year's carpet of dead leaves. There was that joyful thrill of spring in the air, that resurrection of Nature when the thraldom of winter is over, and beauty comes back to the gray dim world. The old Greeks felt it, thousands of years ago, and fabled it in their myth of Persephone and her return from Hades. The Druids knew it in Ancient Britain, and fixed their religious ceremonies for May Day. The birds were caroling it still in the hedgerows, and the girls caught the joyous infection and danced along in defiance of Miss Strong's jog-trot guide walk. Even the mistress herself, so wise at the outset, finally flung prudence to the winds, and skirmished through the coppices with enthusiasm equal to that of her pupils, lured from the pathway by the glimpses of kingcups, or the pursuit of a peacock butterfly.

"All the same, if we tear round like small dogs, we shall never reach Dropwick to-night, and I've booked our rooms there," she assured them. "You don't want to sleep on the heather, I suppose!"

"Bow-wow! Shouldn't mind!" laughed Kitty. "We could cling together and keep each other warm."

"You won't cling to me, thanks! I prefer a bed of my own."

Nora, having brought a good supply of films for her Brownie camera, was most keen on taking snapshots. She photographed the company eating their lunch on a bank by the roadside, with Miss Strong in the very act of biting a piece of bread and butter, and Ingred with her face buried in a mug. She even went further. She had been reading a book on faked photography, and she yearned to try experiments.

"I'm going to give those stay-at-homes a few thrills," she

declared. "I told them we'd have adventures."

Nora expounded her plan to Miss Strong, who was sufficiently interested in the subject to promise her collusion and good advice. A mock Alpine scene came first. Nora had brought with her, for this express purpose, a length of rope, which she wore around her jersey like a Carmelite's girdle. She took it off now and fastened it round the waists of three of her schoolfellows, linking them together in the manner of Swiss mountaineers. Then she found a piece of rock on which were narrow ledges, and, with the help of Miss Strong, posed them in attitudes of apparent peril. Really, they were only a couple of feet from the ground, and a fall would have been a laughing matter, but in a camera they appeared to be clinging almost by their eyelashes to the face of an inaccessible crag and in imminent danger of their lives. Nora took two views, and chuckled with satisfaction.

"That'll make their hair stand on end! I'll fix a few more sensations if I can. Who's game to run six inches in front of a mild old cow's horns, while somebody urges her on from behind?"

"How will you guarantee she's mild?" inquired Bess dubiously. "She might take it into her head to toss us!"

"Not she! It was only the 'cow with the crumpled horn' that went in for tossing."

"Well, I'd rather be in a safer photo, thanks! I'm terrified of cows, anyway."

Nora's instincts were really quite dramatic. She photographed Bess crouching in the hollow of a tree, an imaginary fugitive, to whom Francie, in an attitude of caution, handed surreptitious victuals. She posed Linda, apparently lifeless, on the borders of a pond, with Kitty and Verity applying artificial respiration. She bound up Ingred's head with a handkerchief, and placed her arm in a sling as the result of a fictitious

Angela Brazil

accident, and would have arranged a circle of weeping girls round the prostrate body of Miss Strong, had not that stalwart lady stoutly objected.

"I'm not going to do anything of the sort, so put up that camera, and come along at once. We've wasted far too much time already, and we shall have to step out unless we want to finish our walk in the dark. I promise you tea at Ryton-on-the-Heath, if you hurry, but we can't stop half an hour there unless you put your best foot foremost, so, quick march!"

# CHAPTER XVII

## THE RIVALS

This book does not propose to extol an ideal heroine, only to chronicle the deeds and thoughts of a girl, who, like most other girls, had her pleasant and her disagreeable moods, her high aspirations and good intentions, and her occasional bursts of bad temper. Ingred had been very passionate as a child, and, though she had learnt to put on the curb, sometimes that uncomfortable lower self would take the bit between its teeth and gallop away with her. It is sad to have to confess that the enjoyment of her walking tour was entirely spoilt by an ugly little imp who kept her company. In plain words she was horribly jealous of Bess. Ingred liked to be popular. She was gratified to be warden of "The Pioneers" and a member of the School Parliament. She felt she had an acknowledged standing not only in her own form but throughout the college. Her official position, her cleverness in class, her aptitude for music, her skill at games, made her an all-round force and a referee on most subjects. There is no doubt that Ingred would have had the undivided post of favorite in her form had it not been for Bess Haselford. Not that Bess was in any way a self-constituted rival - on the contrary she was rather shy and retiring, and made no particular bid for popularity. Perhaps that was one reason why the girls liked her. She was generous in lending her property, invited her form-mates to charming parties at Rotherwood, and often persuaded an indulgent father to include some of her special chums in motoring expeditions on Saturday afternoons. She had, indeed, taken up the exact role

Angela Brazil

that Quenrede had played years ago, before the war, and which Ingred would have followed had Rotherwood and a car still been in the Saxons' possession. In spite of several overtures from Bess, Ingred had thrust away all idea of friendship, and had steadily refused any invitations to her old home. The reports which the girls brought back of the renewed glories of Rotherwood made her feel like a disinherited princess. She onsidered it rough luck that her supplanter should be at the same school and in the same form as herself, and decided that Bess had ousted her from both house and favor. It made it only the more aggravating that Bess's musical talent was quite equal, if not superior, to her own. Bess had improved immensely on the violin, and her performance at the end-of-term recital had received quite a little ovation.

When the question of the walking tour was broached, Bess, owing to home engagements, had at first reluctantly refused, then had managed to rearrange her holidays and had joined the party after all. To Ingred her presence utterly marred the enjoyment. It was extremely unreasonable of Ingred, for Bess was most unassuming and really very long-suffering. She put up with snubs that would have made most girls retaliate indignantly. Nobody likes to be sat upon too hard, however, and even the proverbial worm will turn at last.

As the walking party, much urged by Miss Strong straggled along towards Ryton-on-the-Heath, Bess made a lightning dive up a bank and came back with a blue flower plainly of the *labiate* species.

"Bugle!" she remarked with satisfaction.

"Bugle?" echoed Ingred scornfully. "Shows how much you know about botany! That's self-heal!"

"Oh no; it's certainly bugle."

"I tell you it's self-heal. I found some at Lynstones last August and looked it up in the flower-book."

"Very likely you did, but that doesn't prove that this is self-heal."

"It does, for anybody with a pair of eyes. I've been studying botany."

"And so have I!"

"You may think you know everything, Bess Haselford, but you don't know this."

"I didn't say I knew everything; but I'm certain this is bugle all the same, and I stick to it!"

Bess's usually sweet voice had an obstinate note in it for once. She seemed determined to defend her botanical trenches.

"Go it - hammer and tongs!" laughed Kitty. "I'll back the winner!"

"And I'll take the case into court," said Linda, snatching the flower from her schoolfellow's hand and running on to show it to Miss Strong, who was an authority on the subject.

The mistress paused to let the others overtake her.

"Bugle, certainly," she decided emphatically. "The first bit we've found this year. It's out early. Self-heal? Oh dear no! The two are rather alike and are sometimes mistaken one for another, but no botanist would dream of confusing them. Bugle is a spring and early summer flower, and self-heal blooms much later. Make a note in your nature diaries that you found bugle on 15th April."

Considerably squashed, Ingred had for once to acknowledge her botany to be at fault, and, though Bess did not triumph, Francie gave Kitty a poke and the pair giggled.

"Well, of course, one can't be always right," said Ingred airily.

"So it seems; though some people set themselves up for wiseacres!" sniggered Kitty.

Ingred fell behind with Verity and let the others walk on. It was only a trifling incident, but she was annoyed to notice how openly and instantly the girls had sided with Bess. She felt too glum for speech, and as Verity was tired and disinclined to talk, they tramped along in silence.

They had been winding steadily uphill for some miles and were now on the heath from which Ryton took its name. The ground fell steeply to the west, showing glimpses of a great river in the valley below, where the still-leafless woods had burst here and there into faint tokens of spring. Beyond the river rose the characteristic grey hills of the neighborhood, with their stone walls and sheepfolds and stretches of moorland, looking a little hazy in the afternoon light, but with patches of yellow gorse catching the sunshine. Ryton was a delightful little village. Its cottages, built long ago by local craftsmen, seemed absolutely in harmony with the landscape: walls, dormers, and mullions and long undulating roofs were all of limestone and conveyed an impression of sturdy self-respect. The rain worn, lichen-covered roofs had weathered to charming irregularities of form and lovely tones of color. Ivy and clematis climbed over the porches and twisted themselves round the low chimneys. The little gardens were bright with daffodils, mezereon, and flowering currant.

To the girls, somewhat tired and decidedly hungry, the main focus of the village was a long iron post which stretched out over the street and supported a rudely-painted sign of a bird, whose species might have been a puzzle to an ornithologist but for the words "Pelican Inn" that appeared beneath it.

In the long-ago days before railroads, the little hostelry had been a stopping-place for stage-coaches, and a wooden board still set forth that it supplied "Posting in all its branches." The landlord would no doubt have been much dismayed if any wag had entered and demanded a chaise and post-horses to drive to

Gretna Green, and a shabby motor in his stable-yard showed that he marched with the times.

Miss Strong, on consulting her watch, decided that her party might safely indulge in a halt of half an hour, and ordered tea for nine persons. The inn, built on a type common in the district, was entered by an archway leading straight into a courtyard. A door on the right led to the bar, and a door on the left to the coffee-room. To this latter more aristocratic quarter Miss Strong conducted her pupils. Some of them had never before been in a small village hostelry, and were much amused at the quaint old parlor with its sporting prints, its glass cases of stuffed squirrels and badgers, and its horsehair-seated chairs with crochet antimacassars hung over the backs. The atmosphere was certainly rather redolent of stale beer and tobacco, but a bunch of crimson wall-flowers on the table did their best to spread a pleasant perfume. The tea, when, after much delay, it arrived, was delicious. The Pelican was a farm as well as an inn, and the rosy-faced servant girl carried in cream, fresh butter, and red-currant jam to the coffee-room. She apologized for the absence of cake, but it was an omission that nobody minded. Upland air gives good appetites, and, though Miss Strong reminded her flock that this was only a meal by the way, and that supper was ordered for them at Dropwick, they set to work as if they would taste nothing more till midnight. There was something so delightfully fresh and out of the common in having tea at a wayside inn; they felt true pilgrims of the road, and civilization and school seemed to have faded into a far background. The love of travel is in the blood of both Celt and Anglo-Saxon; our forefathers visited shrines for the joy of the journey as well as for religious motives, and maybe our Bronze Age ancestors, who flocked to the great Sun Festivals at Stonehenge or Avebury Circles, derived pleasure from the change of scene as well as a blessing from the Druids. The Romans, those great pioneers of travel, had opened out the district eighteen centuries ago, and laid a straight, paved road from Wendcester to Pursborough; the remains of their fortified camps and of their villas were still left to mark their era. The foss-way, leading from Ryton-on-the-

Angela Brazil

Heath to Dropwick, was their handiwork, and our pilgrims were to march on the identical track of some old Roman legion.

It must be owned that when tea was finished they were very unwilling pilgrims, and would gladly have spent the night at The Pelican and have slept in the funny, musty, low-ceiled little bedrooms upstairs.

"Couldn't we possibly stop here?" implored Verity.

But Miss Strong, having booked rooms in Dropwick, was adamant.

"Besides which I wouldn't trust the beds here," she remarked. "So early in the year they're almost bound to be damp, and we don't want any of you laid up with rheumatic fever as the result of our trip. I prefer to give a wayside inn a week's notice if I mean to sleep there in April. Nobody has had enough coal during the winter to keep fires going in spare bedrooms. That front room was as chilly as a country church! You won't feel so tired, Verity, when you're on your feet again, and it's all downhill to Dropwick."

The Temperance Hotel, where the girls finally stayed their weary feet, was quite modern and unromantic, though well aired and fairly comfortable. Ingred, whom the fates had placed to sleep with Nora, had a trying night, for her obstreperous bedfellow had a habit of flinging out her arms, and of appropriating the larger half of the clothes, leaving poor Ingred to wake shivering. Also, the bed sloped towards the middle, so that both girls had to poise themselves on a kind of hillside, and were constantly rolling down and colliding. These troubles, however, were only incidental in the Pilgrimage, and certainly might have been worse.

On comparing notes at breakfast nearly everybody had had similar experiences. Miss Strong confessed to a patent mattress with a broken spring jutting up in the center, round which she had been obliged to lie in a curve. Linda and Francie had slept near the water-cistern, which alarmed them with weird noises, and Bess and Kitty, trying to open their window wider, had found it lacked sash-cords, and descended like a guillotine, sending the prop that had upheld it, flying into the street. Though they groused at the time, the girls laughed as they discussed these details over the eggs and bacon. The sun was shining and they felt rested, and quite ready once more to shoulder their kit and set out on the march.

There was nothing of very great interest to see in Dropwick itself, though it was a quaint enough old-fashioned market-town, with a fifteenth-century church tower, and a few black and white houses. Miss Strong decided not to waste any time there, but to push on as fast as possible across the hills to Sudbury, where there was a fine Romano-British villa that was well worth a visit. So the foss-way took them up, and up, and up, through fir-woods where the new cones were showing like candles on Christmas trees, and alongside a quarry where they pounced upon some quite interesting fossils in the heaps of stones by the road, and over a craggy weather-worn peak, where, again, they caught the magnificent view of the valley and the river and hills beyond. Then down again, through more fir-woods, where the timber was being felled, and great tree-trunks lay piled in rows one above another, and past banks that were a dream, with starry blackthorn blossom and primroses growing beneath, to where the cross-roads met and the signpost pointed an arm to Sudbury.

The Romans might take their roads straight as an arrow across moor and hill, but they chose out the beauty spots of the land on which to build their villas, and were careful to fix upon a southern aspect and shelter from the prevailing winds. The remains of the old settlement lay behind a farm, and had been carefully excavated by a local antiquarian society. Visitors applied at the farmhouse, entered their names in a book, paid their admission money, and were escorted round by a guide.

Time, and successive conquests, had demolished the greater

part of the villa, but its foundations and some of the old brick walls could be plainly traced. The great bath, that indispensable feature of a Roman establishment, could still be seen, with its beautiful tesselated pavement, inlaid with mosaics of doves, cupids, and designs of fruit and flowers. The heating system also, with the leaden pipes and remains of furnaces, was a testimony to the civilization of the period, and the amount of comfort that the legions brought with them into their foreign exile. A large shed had been fitted up as a museum, and held a number of objects that had been dug up during the excavations. The girls, poring over the glass cases, looked with interest at a Roman lady's silver hand-mirror, toilet pots, and tiny shears that must have been the early substitute for scissors. More fascinating still were the toys from a little child's grave, small glass bottles, roughly-made animals of clay, and a carved object that no doubt had been at one time a treasured doll, though now it was crumbling into dust.

Among the pile of broken statues or fragments of ornamental stonework in the corner was a monumental tablet, cracked across in two places, but pieced together for preservation with iron rivets. The inscription ran:

"D.M. Simpliciae Florentinae Animae Innocentissimae quae vixit menses decem. Felicius Simplex Pater fecit. Leg. vi, V."

(To the Divine Shades. To Simplicia Florentina, a most innocent soul, who lived ten months. Felicius Simplex of the Sixth Legion, the Victorious, the father, erected this.)

Some of the girls glanced at the tablet, and the English translation of the inscription which lay near, and turned away without much notice. But Ingred stood gazing at them with a catch in her throat. They brought a whole pathetic human story to life again. She could picture the noble Roman father, leader of the victorious legion, sent over from Italy and making his home here in a conquered foreign land, as our officers do in India, and bringing with him his lady with her Roman customs and her slaves. Those few brief words - "a most innocent soul who lived ten months" - told the tragedy of the cherished little daughter whose frail life faded in the fogs of the British climate about eighteen hundred years ago. Hearts are the same all the world over, and the pretty dark-eyed Roman baby must have been laid to its rest with as much grief and sadness as the fair-haired darlings whom British mothers sometimes bury in Indian soil.

"It's a sweet name, too - Simplicia Florentina!" mused Ingred. "I wonder what she would have grown up like. And what her history would have been! I'd give worlds to know more about her!"

"Aren't you coming, Ingred?" called Verity from the doorway. "Miss Strong says we ought to be getting on now."

Ingred brought her thoughts back with an effort to the twentieth century, and joined the waiting party outside. Miss Strong was talking to their guide, who was describing a short cut across the fields that would save them several miles on their way to Pursborough.

Verity, after calling to her friend in the museum, had run out. Ingred followed her, to find her with her arm locked closely through Bess's. There was no reason why she should not display such a mark of affection, but to Ingred it seemed little short of an insult to herself. Verity, her particular chum, to have openly gone over to the enemy! She stared at her in surprise. Verity did not appear to notice the stare, however, and walked on quite calmly.

Miss Strong had decided that they should find a quiet place along the lane where they could eat their lunch before beginning the second part of their march. She fixed on a lovely spot with a high wooded bank at the back and in front fields that sloped to the river. There were specks of yellow in these fields, and Kitty who finished her sandwiches first, ran to inspect nearer and reported cowslips. Instantly most of the

Angela Brazil

girls went scrambling over the stile.

Miss Strong, who had bought picture-postcards of the Roman villa, and was addressing them with a stylo-pen, did not follow the exodus. She called to Ingred, however, who was last.

"Warn the girls," she said, "not on any account to go into that meadow where there is a horse with a young foal. The guide at the farm said it is a savage beast and will attack people. Be sure to tell them *all!*"

"I'll run after them now," answered Ingred, calling "Cuckoo!" to attract their attention.

She told Belle and Linda and Verity, who were near to the stile, and Linda passed the news on to Francie and Kitty. Bess was quite a long distance down the field, gathering blackthorn from the hedge.

"I'm not going to tear all that way after her!" thought Ingred crossly. "Verity will be sure to tell her. They seem inseparable to-day. Besides which nobody's particularly likely to go into that other meadow. There are plenty of cowslips here."

It took Miss Strong a much longer time to write her postcards than she had originally intended, and while she was thus employed her girls spread themselves out in quest of flowers. It is always amazing when you start rambling in company with others how quickly you can find yourself alone. By the time Ingred had gathered a fragrant, sweet-smelling bunch and looked round for somebody to admire it, her schoolmates were gone. She hunted about for them, and noticed Verity's green jersey and Kitty's brown tam-o'-shanter in the wood above. Surely they must all be up there together.

She was just going to follow, when a qualm of conscience seized her. She had not delivered Miss Strong's message to Bess, and it would perhaps be as well to ascertain that the latter had not strayed unwarned into the danger zone.

"It's not at all likely," Ingred kept repeating to herself, as she walked briskly along the meadow to the fence. "I'm really only going on a wild goose chase."

Likely or unlikely, it was the very thing which had happened. The cowslips on the other side of the railings were larger and finer, and Bess, having no fear of horses, had climbed over and wandered some way down the field. Only about twenty yards from her the lanky foal was gambolling round its mother, a big draught mare, cropping the grass innocently enough at present, and apparently not perceiving trespassers.

If Bess could retreat quietly and unnoticed from the field all might be well. Ingred did not dare to call for fear of attracting the mare's attention. If Bess would only turn round she might wave to her. But Bess kept her back to the fence and had no idea of danger. There was only one course open to Ingred. She slipped over the railings and went along the meadow to warn her schoolfellow. In a few quiet words she explained the situation.

"Don't run," she whispered. "Let us walk back and perhaps it will take no notice of us."

The girls went as softly as possible, looking over their shoulders every now and then to see that all was safe. Of bulls they had a wholesome terror, but they had had no previous experience of a savage horse.

They were about fifteen yards from the railings, when the mare, which hitherto had been feeding quietly, raised her head and lumbered round. She saw strangers in her territory; her primeval instinct was to protect her foal, and she came tearing across the field with wild eyes and lip turned back from gleaming teeth. The girls fled for their lives. It was a question of which could reach the railings first, they or the dangerous brute whose huge hoofs thundered behind them. Ingred, who was the taller and the stronger of the two, seized Bess by the hand and literally dragged her along. Together they tumbled

Angela Brazil

over the fence somehow and rolled down the bank into the safe shelter of some gorse bushes. For a moment they were afraid the mare would leap after them, but the height of the rails balked her; apparently she was satisfied with routing the enemy and returned across the field to her foal. The girls, with shaking knees, got up and hurried towards the lane where they had left Miss Strong.

"You've saved my life, Ingred!" gasped Bess, as they went along.

"No, I haven't!" choked Ingred. "At least, it was my fault you ever went into the field at all. Miss Strong told me to tell you the horse was savage, and you were such a long way off picking cowslips that I didn't trouble to go after you. I trusted to Verity telling you."

"Verity ran the other way with Kitty."

"I know. Well, at any rate, it was my fault and I'm ready to take the blame. Precious row I shall get into with the Snark!"

"Why should we say anything about it?"

"Not say anything?"

"There's really no need. It's over and done with now. I don't want to get you into a scrape. I vote we just keep it to ourselves."

Ingred paused, with her hand on the gate, and gazed with unaffected astonishment at her companion.

"Bess Haselford, you're the biggest trump I've ever met! It's only one girl in a thousand who'd want to cover up a thing like that. Most people would make *such* a tale of it, and pose as an injured martyr whom I'd nearly murdered. I'm sure Francie would, or even Verity."

"You put yourself into danger to come and warn me!"

"Well, it was the least I could do!"

"Let's forget about it then. And don't tell any of the girls, in case they blab. It would make Miss Strong so nervous, she'd be scared about our going into any fields for ever afterwards."

"Right-o, I won't tell, but I shan't forget. As I said before, I think you're the biggest trump on the face of the earth."

"Cuckoo!" rang out Linda's voice from the bank.

"Where are you girls?" shouted Miss Strong from the lane.

"Coming!" called Ingred, as she latched the gate and hurried with Bess to rejoin the rest of the party.

Angela Brazil

# CHAPTER XVIII

## BESS AT HOME

The Pilgrims, after a glorious tramp down the dale of Beechcombe, reached Pursborough without further adventure, and spent the night there. They gave an hour next morning to inspecting the glorious old church and the ruins of the castle, then once more resumed the Roman road. It was the last day of their tour, so they made the best of it. They explored some delightful woods, followed the course of a fascinating stream, ate their lunch in a picturesque quarry, had an early tea at a wayside inn which rivalled "The Pelican" in quaintness, and finally reached Ribstang in time to catch the 5:20 train to Grovebury. The conclusion of the excursion meant the close of the holiday, for school would begin again on the following Monday. Everybody had enjoyed it immensely, and everybody was only too sorry it was over. To Ingred it marked an epoch. She had suddenly made friends with Bess Haselford. Now she viewed Bess with unprejudiced eyes she realized what an exceedingly nice and attractive girl she really was. The adventure in the field had flung them together, and - much to the astonishment of the others, who did not know their secret - they had walked the whole way from Pursborough to Ribstang in each other's company.

"I can't make out Ingred!" declared Verity. "Here she's been abusing Bess, and calling her a bounder, and now she's hanging on her arm! The way some people turn round is really most extraordinary -"

"'There's naught so queer as folks!'" quoted Linda. "Glad Ingred's come to her senses, at any rate. I always thought she was perfectly beastly to Bess!"

"So she was. I wonder Bess will put up with her now. I'm sure I wouldn't!"

Bess, however, was of a forgiving disposition, and let bygones be bygones. It is the only plan at schools, for girls are generally so frank in the nature of their remarks that if you begin to treasure up the disagreeable things said to you, and let them rankle, you will probably find yourself without a chum in the world. Though the fashion may be for plain speaking, it is often a matter of mood, and the mate who genuinely believes you a "blighter" one day, will claim you as a "mascot" with equal persuasion on the next. It is all part of the wholesome rough-and-tumble of your education, and proves of as much use in training you and rounding your projecting corners as the lessons you learn in your form. The girls thought Ingred's new infatuation would soon wear off, but it had come to stay. She herself was quite surprised at the force of the attraction. It was almost like falling in love. She marched with Bess at drilling, chose her for her partner at tennis, and would have changed desks to sit next to her, had not Miss Strong refused permission. As a natural result of this new state of affairs came a shy invitation from Bess asking Ingred to tea at Rotherwood. After the many previous refusals she would hardly have ventured to give in but for several hints which paved the way. Circumstances, however, alter cases, and Ingred, who had declared that nothing should induce her to set foot in her old home, was now all eagerness to go. She was delighted to find that she was to be the only guest. She felt that on this particular visit even Verity would be *de trop*.

On a certain Tuesday afternoon, therefore, with full permission from Miss Burd, she absented herself from the hostel tea-table, and walked home with Bess instead. It gave her quite a thrill to turn in at the familiar gate of Rotherwood. The lawns were in beautiful order, and the beds gay with

Angela Brazil

tulips, aubrietias, forget-me-nots, and a lovely show of hyacinths. So far from being neglected, the place seemed even better kept than in the old days. The house, with its pretty modern black-and-white front, its many gables, and its cheerful red-tiled roof, looked the same as formerly; but indoors there were great changes. The hall, which used to be Moorish, was now hung with tapestry, and furnished in old oak; the drawing-room was yellow instead of blue, with a big brocade-covered couch and a Chappell piano; the dining-room had rows of book-cases and some good oil-paintings; the morning-room was a cheerful chintz boudoir with a gilt mirror and Chippendale chairs; the conservatory was full of choice flowers, and an aviary had been added to it.

"Mother is so fond of birds," explained Bess. "They amuse her when her head's bad and she doesn't care to see anybody. She's made most of them wonderfully tame."

Mrs. Haselford proved to be a gentle pleasant lady who shook hands kindly with Ingred, then excused herself on the score of ill-health, and retired to her room, leaving the girls to have tea by themselves.

"Mother's never been really well for three years," said Bess. "Not since Bert and Larry -"

She did not finish her sentence, but her eyes turned to the wall where hung two portraits of lads in khaki. Ingred understood. She knew that Bess had lost both brothers in the war, and she had heard that poor Mrs. Haselford had shut herself up in her grief and refused all comfort, sometimes even to the extent of remaining for days upstairs, and neglecting the company of husband and child. Her attitude to Bess was often peculiar, it was almost as if she resented her daughter being left when her adored boys had been taken from her. Bess never knew how she would be received, for sometimes her mother would seem unable to bear her presence, and at other times would unreasonably chide her for neglect. It began to dawn on Ingred how very lonely her friend must be. She had secretly envied her the possession of Rotherwood, but now she realized how little the house itself would mean without the happy home life in which brothers and sister had borne their part.

"I'd rather have the bungalow with the family, than Rotherwood all alone!" she ruminated. "As for Muvkins, she's one in a million. I believe she'd be cheery in a coal cellar, so long as she'd a solitary chick to keep under her wing. Why, if we'd lost *our* boys, she'd have been trying to make it up to Queenie and me for not having brothers. I know her! That's her way!"

Bess had much to show to her visitor when tea in the dainty morning-room was over. There were her books, and her photographs and postcard albums, and all kinds of girlish possessions, and a cocker spaniel with three puppies as fat as roly-poly puddings, and a fern-case opening out of one of her bedroom windows, and a collection of pressed wild flowers, and a green parroquet that would sit on her wrist, and allow her to stroke its head, though it snapped at strangers. They had been working upwards through the house, and finally Bess led the way to the top landing of all. She paused for a moment before the door of an attic room.

"I expect you'll know this place!" she remarked shyly, ushering in her guest.

Ingred looked round in amazement. It was a little sanctum which she and Quenrede had shared in the old days as a kind of studio. Here they had been allowed to try experiments in poker work, painting, fret-carving, spatter-work, or any other operations which were considered too messy to be performed in the school-room downstairs. They had loved their "den," as they called it, and had taken a particular pleasure in covering its walls with pictures, cut, most of them, from magazines, and stuck on with glue or paste. During the occupation of Rotherwood by the "Red Cross," this room had been locked up, and Ingred had imagined that Mr. Haselford would have had it papered when the rest of the house was decorated. She

Angela Brazil

was delighted to find it in this untouched condition. All her dear former treasures adorned the walls, and she ran from one to another rejoicing over them. There was even a further surprise. Years ago an artist cousin had sketched her portrait in pastel crayons upon the color-wash of the wall. It had been done as a mere artistic freak, but like many such spontaneous drawings it had been an admirable likeness and a very pretty picture. It bore her name, "Ingred," in flourishy letters underneath. The whole of this had now been protected with a sheet of glass and enclosed by a frame. A table in the room, an easy chair, and a gas-fire seemed to point to its occasional occupation.

"You actually haven't had this changed!" exclaimed Ingred. "I thought it must all have been swept away by now!"

"No. You see, Father took me over the house when first he decided to come here, and when he was arranging what papers to choose. I fell in love with this dear wee room just as it was, and begged that it mightn't be touched. Father let me have it for my very own. It was so different from all other rooms. I liked the pictures pasted on the walls, and the bits of poker-work nailed up. I knew some other girls must have been here, and it gave me a homely feeling, as if you had only gone away for a few minutes, and might come back any time and talk to me. Then there was your portrait. I wondered who 'Ingred' was! The name struck my fancy immensely, and so did the face. You remember we removed to Rotherwood at the end of July, and all the rest of the summer I wondered about the portrait. I used to come up here and sit when I felt very lonely, and it seemed company, somehow. You can't think how fond I got of it. I suppose I was rather silly and absurd, but I knew nobody in Grovebury then, and Mother was ill in her room, and Father away all day - anyhow I got into the habit of talking to it as if it were a girl friend, and showing it my paintings, and my pressed flowers, and everything I was doing. I pretended it liked to see them. Sometimes I even brought up my violin and played to it. That was nicer than being quite by myself. It grew to be as dear to me as the little sister I had always longed to have.

"Then in September I went to the College. You can imagine what a start it gave me when somebody called you 'Ingred.' I looked at you, and I saw at once that you were the 'Ingred' of my picture, only grown older. I was absolutely thrilled. It was very foolish of me, but I thought somehow you'd understand. Of course you didn't! How could you? It was idiotic of me to expect it. The 'Ingred' on the wall was simply the friend of my fancy."

"And the real one was just hateful to you!" said Ingred sorrowfully. "I know I was a perfect beast! I was ashamed of myself all the time, only I wouldn't confess it. Lispeth used to slate me sometimes for my nastiness. She called me 'a jealous blighter,' and so I was! The girl of your fancy is a great deal nicer than I am, or ever can be, but I'll try to live up to her as well as I can, Bess, if you'll let me!"

"Let you!" echoed Bess, linking her arm affectionately in that of her friend. "You're a perfect dear nowadays."

The girls tore themselves away quite regretfully from the little attic studio, but time was passing only too quickly, and they wished to try a game of tennis before Ingred returned to the hostel.

"So you like the house in its new dress?" asked Bess as they walked down the steps into the garden. "Father thinks it's beautiful. He says Mr. Saxon is the best architect he knows. He's simply put every thing in exactly the right place. Does he only design houses, or does he go in for anything bigger?"

"He would if he got the chance," replied Ingred. "What sort of things do you mean?"

"Oh, a church, or a museum, or an art gallery."

"I know he's done most splendid designs for these, but he's

never had the luck to get them accepted. There's generally so much influence needed to get your plans taken for a big public building like that. At least, that's what Dad says. If you have a relation on the City Council, it makes a vast difference to your chances. We've no friends at Court."

"Oh!" said Bess, rather abstractedly, and the subject dropped.

The girls had only time for one game of tennis, when the stable-clock, chiming half-past six, reminded Ingred that if she wished to do her preparation that evening she must rush back to the hotel. She bade Bess a reluctant good-by.

"You'll come and see me again?" asked the latter.

"Rather! And I'll send thought-waves to animate my portrait, and let it talk for me in my absence," laughed Ingred. "Perhaps you'll get more than you bargain for - I'm an awful chatter-box."

"You'll never talk too much for me," said Bess, as she kissed her good-by.

# CHAPTER XIX

## THE NUN'S WALK

The Saxon family agreed that whatever might be the drawbacks of Wynch-on-the-Wold in wintry weather, it was an idyllic spot in the month of May. The wall-flowers which Ingred had transplanted were now in their prime, the apple trees were in blossom, clumps of lilies were pushing up fast, and pink double daisies bordered the front walk. The woods in the combe below the moor were a mass of bluebells, and here and there those who searched might find rarer flowers, orchises, lily of the valley, and true lover's knot. Friends who had shirked the journey while the winds blew cold, now began to drop in at the bungalow and take tea under the apple trees. Ingred, returning home on Friday afternoons, would find bicycles stacked by the gate and visitors seated in the garden. She greeted them with enthusiasm or the reverse, according to her individual tastes.

"Really, Ingred, they don't seem to teach manners at the College now!" said Quenrede one day.

"The way you scowled at Mrs. Galsworthy and Gertrude was most uncivil. You didn't look in the very least pleased to see them."

"I wasn't! They're the most stupid people on the face of the earth! And they stayed such ages. I thought they'd never go. Just when I wanted a nice private talk with you and Mother before the boys came back. Why should you look glad to see a person when you're not?"

"For the sake of manners, my dear!"

"Then manners really mean humbug," declared Ingred, who loved to argue. "To say you're glad to see people, when you're not, is telling deliberate fibs. Most hypocritical, I call it! Why can't people tell the truth?"

"Because it would generally be offensive and unkind to do so," put in Mother, who happened to overhear. "There's another side to the question, too. When you say - against your will - that you are glad to see somebody, you mean that all the *best* part of you is glad - the kind, generous part that likes to give pleasure, not the selfish lower part that only thinks of its own convenience. So you are not really telling a fib, but being true to your nobler self. A great deal of what people call 'plain speaking' is simply giving rein to their most uncharitable thoughts. As a rule, I say Heaven defend me from those ultra-truthful souls who enjoy 'speaking their minds.'"

"But are we to gush over every bore?" asked Ingred.

"There are limits, of course. We can't let all our time be frittered away by idle friends, but we can generally manage tactfully without offending them. Don't look so woe-begone, childie! Nobody else is coming to-night, and I promise you tea in the woods to-morrow."

"By ourselves?"

"Unless anyone very nice comes over to join us," put in Quenrede quickly.

"You girls shall give the invitations. I won't bring any middle-aged people," laughed Mother, with a sly glance at Quenrede.

The party in the bluebell woods on Saturday was entirely a

family one, with the exception of Mr. Broughten, who rode over on a motor-bicycle ostensibly to lend some microscopic slides to Athelstane, though Ingred suspected there was another attraction in the visit. Quenrede, who professed great surprise, gave him a guarded welcome.

"After all the fuss you made about my manners yesterday, you might have seemed more glad to see him," sniffed Ingred critically.

"Might I? Well, really, I think I'm going to hang a label round my neck: 'Pleased to meet you! Let 'em all come!' It would save trouble. Stick tight to me when we're gathering bluebells. Three's better company sometimes than two. Don't I like him? Oh yes, he's all right, but I'm not keen on a *tete-a-tete.*"

After which hint, Ingred, who had some acquaintance with the perversity of Quenrede's feminine mind, did exactly the opposite, and, abandoning her basket to the custody of Mr. Broughten, left him helping her sister to gather bluebells, and took herself off with Hereward.

"He's not half bad!" she ruminated laughingly. "Not of course a fairy prince exactly, or even a Member of Parliament, but the bubbles on the pool by the whispering stones certainly came to 'J,' and his name is 'John,' for I asked Athelstane. There's the finger of fate about it, and Queenie had better make up her mind."

With Ingred, however, school matters were at present much more interesting than speculating about her sister's possible future. It was an interesting term at the College. Cricket and tennis were in full swing, and she took an active part in both. The best of being at the hostel was that the boarders had the benefit of the tennis courts in the evening, and so secured an advantage in the matter of practice over any girls who did not possess a private court at home. So far the College had not competed in tournaments, but Blossom Webster was hopeful that later on in the term some champions might be chosen who would not disgrace the Games Club. Meantime she urged everybody to practice, and coached her favorites with the eye of an expert. Nora was particularly marked out for future distinction. She had made tremendous strides lately, and her swift serves were the terror of her opponents. The hostel felt justly proud of her achievements, and would collect in the evening, after prep., to watch her play a set of singles with Susie Wakefield, who, though older and taller, almost invariably lost.

Susie had good points of her own, however, and with Nora as partner could beat even Blossom and Aline occasionally. No doubt the future credit of the school was in their hands.

One evening it happened that Nora was in a particularly slashing and reckless mood, and she sent no less than three balls flying straight over the wall that bordered the tennis courts. They fell into the premises of old Dr. Broadfield, whose garden adjoined that of the school. They were not the first that had done so, indeed so many balls had gone over lately that the loss was growing serious. At one time the girls had been wont to ring Dr. Broadfield's front-door bell and beg permission to pick up their property, but they had been received so sourly by his elderly housekeeper, that they hardly dared to ask again.

"Three good balls gone in half an hour!" grieved Verity. "There'll soon be none left at this rate. I believe there must be a dozen at least lying on the grass over there, only that stingy old thing won't throw them back. It's really too bad."

"How could we possibly get them?" ruminated Doreen.

"Sham ill, get Dr. Broadfield to attend, and coax them out of him," suggested Fil.

Doreen shook her head.

"He's not the school doctor, unfortunately. When Millie

sprained her ankle, Miss Burd sent for Dr. Harrison. We might fish for them with a butterfly net tied to the end of a drilling pole, if they're anywhere near enough."

"They're not. I peeped over the wall and they've rolled quite a long way off."

"How weak! What are we to do?"

"There's nothing for it," said Ingred slowly, "but to make a sally into the enemy's trenches and fetch them back!"

"Oh! I dare say! But who's going to do the sallying business?"

"*I* will, if you like."

"*You!*"

"Yes; I don't mind a scrap."

"You heroine!"

"Don't mensh!"

"But suppose you're caught?"

"I shall have to risk that, of course. I'll reconnoiter carefully first."

The boundary between the College premises and the property of Dr. Broadfield was part of the old Abbey wall. The mortar had crumbled away from the stones, leaving large interstices, so it was quite easy to climb. With a little boosting from Verity and Nora, Ingred successfully reached the top, and peered over into the neighboring garden. Just below her was a rockery, which offered not only an easy means of descent, but a quick mode of egress in the case of the necessity of beating a hasty retreat.

Beyond the flower-bed, and lying on the lawn, were no less than seven tennis balls, marked with the unmistakable blue cross that claimed them for the College. The sight was enough to spur on the faintest heart. Apparently there was nobody in this part of the garden, and no watchful face peered from any of the windows. It was certainly an opportunity that ought not to be missed. Ingred slipped first one foot and then the other over the wall, and dropped on to the rockery. It was the work of a minute to pick up the balls and throw them back to rejoicing friends. If she herself had followed immediately there would have been no sequel to the episode. But happening to look under the bushes, she noticed another ball, and went in quest of it. It seemed a shame to return until she had found any that might have strayed farther afield, so she dived under the rhododendron bushes, and was rewarded with two more balls. She had issued out on to another part of the lawn, and was on the very point of retreating, when she suddenly heard voices on the path between the bushes. To run to the wall would be to cross open country, so, with an instinctive desire to seek cover, she dived into a summer-house close by, and shut the door. The footsteps came nearer. Were they going to follow her into her retreat, and catch her? It would be too ignominious! Peeping warily through a small window of the summer-house, she saw two young people, apparently much interested in each other, strolling leisurely up. To her immense relief they did not attempt to enter, but sat down on a seat outside the window. They were so near that she could perforce hear every word, and was an unwilling but compulsory eavesdropper.

At first the conversation consisted mostly of tender nothings: "He" certainly called her "Darling!"; "She" replied: "Oh, Donald, don't!" and a sound followed so suspiciously like a kiss that Ingred, only a few feet away from them, almost giggled aloud. She wondered how long they were going to keep her a prisoner. It might be very pleasant for themselves to sit "spooning" in the garden on a mild May evening, but if they prolonged their enjoyment beyond eight o'clock, the hostel supper-bell would ring, and any girl not in her place at the table would lose a mark for punctuality.

"He" on the other side of the window, was waxing sentimental about old times and bygone days.

"I'm glad you're not a nun, darling!" he remarked fatuously. "If you had lived in the ancient Abbey, I shouldn't have been able to walk about the garden with you, should I?"

"I suppose not," she ventured, "especially if you'd been a monk."

"I dare say some of them *did* manage to do a little love-making sometimes, though. What's that story about the ghost?"

"The White Nun, do you mean? The one that haunts the College gardens?"

(Ingred pricked up her ears at this).

"Yes. Isn't there some legend or other about her?"

"I believe there is, but I've forgotten it. I only know she walks on moonlight nights, down the steps by the sun-dial, and then disappears into the wall near the Abbey. At least she's supposed to. I've never met anybody who's seen her. Don't talk of such shuddery things! You make me feel creepy!"

Apparently he offered masculine protection, for another suggestive sound was followed by a giggle and a remonstrance. The hostel bell was ringing, and the Abbey clock was striking eight. Were they going to stay talking all night? Ingred was growing desperate. She wondered how she was going to explain her absence to Mrs. Best. She even debated whether it would be advisable to open the summer-house door, bolt across the lawn, and trust to luck that the matter was not reported at the College. She had her hand on the latch when the feminine voice outside remarked:

Angela Brazil

"It's getting chilly, Donald!"

"Don't catch cold, darling!" with tender solicitude. "Would you rather go indoors?"

"Hooray!" triumphed Ingred inwardly, though she did not dare to utter a sound.

It took a little while for the lovers to get under way and finally stroll back along the path among the bushes. Ingred gave them time to walk out of sight and hearing, then made a dash for the rockery, scrambled over the wall, tore across the tennis courts, and entered the dining-room nearly ten minutes late for supper. Mrs. Best looked at her reproachfully, and Doreen, who was monitress for the month, took a notebook from her pocket and made an entry therein. Nora and Verity and Fil went on eating sago blanc-mange with stolid countenances that betrayed no knowledge of their room-mate's doings, but that night, when The Foursomes met in the privacy of Dormitory 2, they demanded an account of her adventure.

She certainly had a piece of interesting news to confide.

"Did you know that a ghost haunts the garden?"

"No! Oh, I say, where?"

"That part by the sun-dial. I've heard it called 'The Nun's Walk!'"

"So have I; but I never knew there was a ghost!"

"It's supposed to walk on moonlight nights."

"How fearfully thrillsome!"

"I've never seen a ghost!" shivered Fil.

"No more have I - and I've never met anyone who exactly has.

It's generally their cousin's cousin who's told them about it."

"There's a moon to-night," remarked Nora.

"So there is!"

The four girls looked at one another, hair brushes in hand. Each had it on the tip of her tongue to make a suggestion.

"I *dare* you to go!" said Verity at last.

"Not alone?"

Fil was clutching already at Nora's hand.

"Well, no! Hardly alone. I vote we all go together and try if we can see anything."

"It would be rather spooksomely jinky!"

"Well, look here, don't let's undress properly, but get into bed, and cover ourselves up until Nurse has been her rounds, then we'll slip downstairs and out through the side door into the garden. Are you game?"

"Who's afraid?" said Ingred valiantly.

Upstairs in their bedroom, with the gas turned on, it was easy enough to feel courageous. Their spirits rose indeed at the prospect of such an adventure. Nurse Warner, who came into the room a little later, looked round at the four beds, turned out the gas, and departed without a suspicion. She had not been gone five minutes when a surreptitious dressing took place, and four figures in dark coats stole down the stairs. Though the building of the College might be absolutely modern, the garden was a relic of mediaeval days. It had formerly belonged to the nunnery of St. Mary's, and had adjoined the Abbey. Parts of the crumbling old wall were still left, and a flagged path led from a sun-dial to some ruins. In the day-time it was a cheerful place, and a blaze of color. The girls had never before seen it in its night aspect. On this May evening it had a quiet beauty that was most impressive. The full moon shone on the great dark pile of the Abbey towers and the beech avenue beyond. There was just light enough in the garden to distinguish bushes as heavy masses, and to trace the paths from the grass. The air was sweet with the scent of flowers.

It is amazing how different conditions can alter a scene: at noon, with the hum from the busy streets, it was common-place enough; by moonlight it became a mystic bower of enchantment. The girls walked along very quietly, treading on the grass so as to make no noise. A slight mist was rising from the ground near the Abbey; in the rays of the moon it resembled a lake. Everything, indeed, was altered. The outline of the sumach bush was like a crouching tiger; the laburnum tassels waved like skeleton fingers. It seemed a witching, unreal world.

Four rather scared girls crept along, clasping hands for moral support. Each secretly would have been relieved to abandon the quest, but did not like to be the first to turn tail. They had determined to walk from the sun-dial to the Abbey wall and back again. So far the garden, though mysterious, showed no signs of anything supernatural. They began to pluck up courage, and even to talk to one another in low whispers. At the ruins they turned and looked back towards the sun-dial. The moonlight streamed along the flagged path, and shimmered on the clumps of early yellow lilies.

What was that, stealing from under the shelter of the hawthorn tree? The girls gasped and almost stopped breathing.

A tall figure, clothed in some long white garment, was gliding towards them. It kept in the shadow, and they could see no details, only a light mass that was slowly and steadily advancing apparently straight to where they were crouching beside the wall. Fil was trembling like a leaf, Nora declared afterward that her hair stood on end, Ingred and Verity felt shivers run down their spines. Nearer and nearer came the white figure. Its approach was more than flesh and blood could stand. With a wild shriek Fil dashed across the lawn, followed closely by Nora, Ingred, and Verity.

"Girls!" cried a clear and well-known voice. "Girls! Stop! What are you doing here?"

There was no mistaking the tone of command of the head-mistress. Four amazed and crestfallen damsels halted and turned back, to find Miss Burd, attired in a white dressing-gown, standing in the moonlight on the grass.

"What is the meaning of this?" she asked. "And why aren't you all in bed?"

It is always difficult to give explanations, and (to such a matter-of-fact person as Miss Burd) it seemed particularly silly to have to confess that they had come out ghost-hunting, and had mistaken her for a spirit. She emptied the vials of her scorn upon their dejected heads.

"Don't let me hear of any more nonsense of this sort!" she finished. "I should have thought you were too intelligent to believe in such rubbish. As for leaving your dormitory at this hour, you deserve to be locked in the cycle-shed for the night. I shall, of course, report you to Mrs. Best, and none of you will play tennis for a week, as a punishment."

Miss Burd, bristling with anger, swept the delinquents before her to the door of the hostel, and watched them flee upstairs, then went to lay the matter before Mrs. Best.

In Dormitory 2, four girls got into bed at topmost speed.

"Of all the ill-luck!" mourned Fil.

"I didn't know Miss Burd prowled about the garden in a

dressing-gown," exclaimed Ingred.

"She *did* look exactly like a ghost!" confirmed Verity.

"Tennis off for a whole week! Blossom will be furious! It's too absolutely grizzly for anything!" groused Nora. "I wish the wretched old ghost had been at Jericho before we went to look for it!"

# CHAPTER XX

## UNDER THE LANTERNS

It is an ill wind that blows nobody good, and though Nora, Fil, Ingred, and Verity might chafe at being debarred from tennis for a whole week, their adventure in the garden had given them an idea. How it exactly originated could not be decided, for each fiercely claimed the full credit for it. Its evolution, however, was somewhat as follows:

Stage 1. How lovely the garden looked in the evening.

Stage 2. Why should we not *all* enjoy it some time?

Stage 3. Miss Burd evidently does.

Stage 4. And looked very fascinating in her white dressing-gown.

Stage 5. It was exactly like a fancy dress.

Stage 6. Why should not we all wear fancy dress?

Stage 7. *Let us ask Miss Burd to let the hostel have a fancy-dress dance in the school garden.*

Great minds generally think in company, and often hit upon the same invention at the same moment, so perhaps all four girls had an equal share in the brain-wave. They communicated it cautiously to companions, and as it "caught on" they sounded Mrs. Best, and finding her favorably disposed to the scheme, begged her to intercede for them with Miss Burd. The head-mistress was wonderfully gracious about the matter, gave full permission for the dance, promised to be present herself, and allowed the invitation to be extended to any mistresses and seniors who would care to join the party. It was quite a long time since the hostel had had any particularly exciting doings, so that the girls flung themselves into their preparation with much enthusiasm. Those who were lucky enough already to possess fancy costumes, or who were able to borrow them, of course scored, and the rest set to work to manufacture anything that came to hand. It was to be in the nature of an impromptu affair, but a few days' notice was given, and the girls were able to devote a Saturday to the all-absorbing problem. Ingred, home for the week-end, enlisted the help of Mother and Quenrede, and turned the bungalow almost upside down in her quest for suitable accessories. She thought of a number of characters she would have liked to impersonate, but was always balked by the lack of some vital article of dress.

"It's no use!" she lamented. "I can't be 'Joan of Arc' without a suit of armor, or 'Queen Elizabeth' when I haven't a flowered velvet robe! I'm so tired of all the old things! It's too stale to twist some roses in my hair for 'Summer,' and I've been a gipsy so often that everybody knows my red handkerchief and gilt beads. I'd as soon be a Red Indian squaw!"

"And why shouldn't you be?" asked Quenrede. "It's a remarkably pretty costume."

"Oh, I dare say, if I could beg, borrow, or steal it!"

"You've no need to do either, my dear. I've had a brain-wave, and we'll fix it up for you at home. Yes, I mean it! Allow me to introduce myself: 'Miss Quenrede Saxon, Court Costumier. The very latest theatrical productions.' I'll make you look so that your own mother will hardly know you!"

"I'd like to puzzle them!" rejoiced Ingred. "Miss Burd said she should have a parade, and hinted something about a prize. They always give points to whoever has the best disguise. Masks are barred, but we may paint our faces. I think I shall be rather choice as a squaw!"

"You ought to have me with you as your 'brave'!" chuckled Hereward.

"It's a 'Ladies Only' dance, so you can't be invited, my boy! There won't be a solitary masculine individual present - even the gardener will have gone home."

"You bet folks will peep in!"

"No, they won't. The premises are strictly private."

Quenrede was in some respects a clever and ingenious little person. She was not much good at ordinary dressmaking, where fashion must be followed, but she displayed great originality in her construction of Ingred's fancy costume. There were two clean sacks in the house, and she commandeered them. She cut one into a skirt and the other into a jumper, stitched up the sides, and frayed out the bottoms to represent fringes. Then she took her water-color paints, mixed them with Chinese white to form a strong body color, and painted Indian patterns on both garments. The head-dress she considered a triumph. She went to a neighboring poultry farm, and boldly begged the tail feathers which had been plucked the day before from some game fowls. These she glued round a cardboard crown, and the effect was magnificent. A dress rehearsal was held, and the family rejoiced over Ingred's most decidedly Wild West appearance.

"You have a pair of real moccasins that Uncle Ernest sent you for bedroom slippers. I'll cut some strips of cloth into fringe for leggings, and you can wear Athelstane's leather belt, and carry an axe for a tomahawk," said Quenrede, surveying her work with critical satisfaction. "Don't forget to paint your face!"

"I shan't show anyone my costume beforehand," chuckled Ingred. "I really don't believe anyone will know me! What luck if I won a prize for the best disguise!"

"Bet you anything you like you don't!" murmured Hereward.

"Why shouldn't I?"

"Because there may be others even better!"

"Well, of course, that's for Miss Burd to judge! But I think I've a sporting chance, at any rate!"

The dance was to be held on Monday evening after supper, when it was just beginning to grow dusk. The mistresses had taken the matter up quite enthusiastically, and had stretched some wires across the garden, and hung up Chinese lanterns. The hostel piano had been pulled close to the window, so that the strains of music could float out into the garden. At least fifteen seniors had accepted the invitation, and it was rumored that Miss Burd had invited a few private friends. Supper was held earlier than usual, so as to allow time for the all-important operation of dressing, and the moment it was finished every inmate of the hostel fled to her bedroom. Dormitory 2 was naturally a scene of much confusion. The girls tried to put on their own costumes and help each other at the same time. Fil, as a Dresden China Shepherdess, needed much assistance in the settling of her panniers, and the arrangement of her curls, which by special permission from Mrs. Best had been twisted up in curl papers from four o'clock until the last available moment, and came out, much to Fil's satisfaction, in quite creditable ringlets. The effect was so altogether charming that her room-mates called a general halt for admiration.

"You look like a mixture of Dolly Varden and Sweet Lavender, with a dash of Maid Marian thrown in," decided Verity.

"I hope my hair'll keep in curl! There's rather a damp feeling in the air," fluttered Fil anxiously.

"You could fly indoors, and give it a twist with the tongs, if it gets very limp," suggested Nora.

Nora herself was going as a personification of "The Kitchen." Her skirt was draped with dusters and dish-cloths, she wore a small dish-cover as a hat, clothes-pegs were suspended round her neck as a necklace, and she brandished a rolling-pin in her hand.

"I'm bound to be something comic," she assured the others. "I'd never keep my face straight for a romantic character. I could no more live up to Lady Jane Grey than I could fly! She's above me altogether!"

Verity, who had borrowed a Dutch costume slightly too small for her, was trying to squeeze her proportions into the tight velvet bodice, and looked dubiously at the sabots.

"I'll never be able to dance in those!" she decided. "I'll put them on to start with, and then kick them off and slip on my sandals instead. They're the most extraordinary clumpy things in the world, I feel like a cat walking in walnut shells!"

Ingred's toilet progressed very favorably till it came to the stage of coloring her face. She was not quite sure as to the best means of obtaining a Red Indian complexion. First she tried rubbing it with soil from the garden, but that was a painful process which almost scraped the skin from her cheeks. So she washed her face and used cocoa. She mixed it in a cup and dabbed it over, but it would not go on smoothly, and the result was so patchy and hideous that once more she brought out her sponge and wiped it off. At that point Verity came to the rescue, smeared the poor cheeks (already sore through such ill-treatment) with vanishing cream, then powdered on some dry cocoa, which certainly gave a dusky and non-European aspect to her features, especially when combined with the

Angela Brazil

feather head-dress. Her dark hair, plaited in two long tails, completed the illusion. The girls held a complacent review of their toilets, then walked downstairs with caution, for Nora's dish-cover was difficult to balance as a hat, and Verity's heels kept slipping out of the sabots. Fil's ringlets, alas! were already beginning to untwist, and Ingred's jumper, put on in too big a hurry, showed symptoms of splitting down the seam. There was no time for repairs of any sort, however. They were five minutes late, and the rest of the company were assembled on the lawn. The boarders from the hostel, together with mistresses and seniors who had come by invitation, made a total of more than fifty persons, all in fancy dress.

These gay costumes were a pretty sight against the background of trees and bushes and flower-beds. The sun had set, leaving a yellow glow in the sky, and the Chinese lanterns were beginning to glow in the gathering twilight. It was certainly a varied crowd; all centuries had met together. A Japanese damsel walked arm-in-arm with a Lancashire witch; an Italian peasant hob-a-nobbed with "The Queen of Sheba," a Spanish lady was talking to "Old Mother Hubbard," while such characters as "A Medicine Bottle," or "An Aeroplane" rubbed shoulders with an "Egyptian Princess" or "Dick Whittington's Cat."

Miss Burd, garbed appropriately as Chaucer's Prioress, received the company at the top of the sun-dial steps, looking, in the opinion of the Foursome League, quite sufficiently like the ghost of yesterday to have justified squeals had they met her alone. When the ceremony of introduction was over, the guests dispersed about the lawn, Miss Perry struck up a waltz on the piano, and the fun began. Dancing on the grass, in the growing darkness, with the Chinese lanterns sending out a soft but uncertain radiance overhead, was a new experience to most of the school. It was difficult not to step on to the flower-beds, or to brush against the bushes. Trailing garments were decidedly in the way, and came to grief. There was a delirious sort of Eastern feeling about it - a kind of combination of "The Thousand and One Nights" and the "Rubaiyat of Omar

Khayyam." The Abbey tower for once seemed out of place, and ought to have changed miraculously into a pagoda or a minaret.

It was after the girls had been dancing for some little time that Ingred first noticed a couple whom she did not remember to have seen before. They followed persistently in her steps, and even gently bumped into her once or twice, thus compelling her attention. She looked at them, considerably mystified. One was attired in Early Victorian Costume, with a crinoline, a little tippet, and a poke bonnet, from which peeped some bewitching ringlets; the other, in a gorgeous Turkish costume, was enveloped in a shimmering gauze veil.

"Who are those?" Ingred asked her partner.

But Verity could not tell.

In the twilight it was, of course, easy to make mistakes, but Ingred began to have a strong suspicion that neither of the mysterious partners belonged to the school. They were certainly not members of the Fifth or Sixth. Perhaps some of the Juniors had forced themselves in? No, they were too tall for Juniors.

"Perhaps they are ghosts!" shivered Verity.

"Ghosts don't bump into people. These are real substantial flesh and blood!"

"It's so dark, we can hardly see."

"Well, I vote we keep close to them, and next time we get near a lantern, we'll turn the tables and bump into them, and try to see who they are."

It was easier said than done, however; the strangers seemed to have changed their tactics, and instead of pursuing Ingred and Verity now endeavored to avoid them. No "elusive

Pimpernels" could have been more difficult to follow. They would come quite close and then suddenly dodge and glide away, only to reappear and repeat the same tantalizing performance. Ingred and Verity began to get on their mettle. It was so evidently done on purpose that they were fully determined to catch the errant pair. After a long game at hide-and-seek they at last managed to dance along side them, and laying violent hands upon them, to drag them into the light of a lantern. As Ingred gazed for a moment in perplexity, the Early Victorian lady gave a most un-Early Victorian wink inside the poke bonnet.

"Hereward! How *dare* you!" gasped his sister.

A firm hand drew her away from the light, and in the shelter of a laurel bush, a voice, choking with laughter, proclaimed:

"Done you, old girl! Done you brown! What about that bet? I told you you'd never know me!"

"You abominable young wretch," replied Ingred, laughing in spite of herself. "How *did* you manage it? And who is your friend?"

"Allow me to introduce Vashti, Queen of Persia!"

"Bunkum! It's a boy! I know it is!"

The explosive sounds issuing from under the shimmering veil of Queen Vashti certainly sounded more masculine than feminine, and that Persian princess confessed presently to the name of Franklin.

"He's a chum of mine," explained Hereward, "and he lives close by, so we made it up to come together. His sister lent us the clothes and dressed us. I say, your Prioress never found us out, did she? What about that prize?"

"There isn't going to be a prize, and you certainly wouldn't have deserved it! Look here, you'd better wangle yourselves off before it gets about who you are. *I* should get into a row, not you!"

"Would the Prioress kick up rough?"

"She'd probably think I'd planned the whole business, and encouraged you to come."

"Even if we apologized?"

"She wouldn't accept an apology. If you want me to have any tennis next week, you had better clear out."

"Just a round with you first, and Franklin can take your friend, or vice versa if you prefer it!"

"You impudent boy! Certainly not. I daren't risk it. Look, Miss Strong is bringing out the lamp, and putting it on the sun-dial, and I believe Miss Perry is going to take a flashlight photo presently. If you want to disgrace me for ever -"

"We'll go!" sighed a mournful voice. "Though it's Adam and Eve turned out of Paradise. I say, Franklin, they don't want us, after all our trouble! We'd better be getting on, I suppose. Our deepest respects to the Prioress. She's given us a delightful evening, if she only knew it. We'd like to come again some time. Ta-ta!"

# CHAPTER XXI

## THE ABBEY RECITAL

Now that Ingred had at last made friends with Bess, she found they had innumerable subjects of interest in common. They were both keen tennis players, dabbled a little in art, pursued Nature study, liked acting, when they had any opportunity of showing their talents in that line, and were enthusiastic over music. Bess was making as good progress on the violin as Ingred on the piano, so there seemed great possibilities of playing together. Sometimes when Bess brought her instrument to school for her lesson, she and Ingred would try over a few pieces, and other girls who chanced to be near would collect and act audience.

"I vote we get up a musical society next year," suggested Ingred. "It's impossible this term - we've too much on our hands already - but if the societies are rearranged in September, we'll agitate to let music take a much bigger place than it has done so far."

"Yes, that would be glorious!" agreed Bess, with visions of a school choir, and even a school orchestra, dancing before her eyes. "Signor Chianti is leaving Grovebury, so if we have a new violin master next term, I hope it will be somebody who's enthusiastic and able and willing to organize things."

"That's the point, of course. Dr. Linton is very able, but not willing to bother with us beyond our lessons - he's so frightfully busy. I suppose he feels that after training the Abbey choir, and conducting choral societies to sing his cantatas, he doesn't care to trouble himself over schoolgirls."

"He's a *real* musician, though. I often wish I could study under him. I'd love to play something with him, just once, to see how it feels to have him accompany me. I think it would be so inspiring, it would just make one let oneself go! I stay every Sunday evening after service at the Abbey to hear his recitals. Occasionally somebody plays the violin, and his accompaniment is simply gorgeous. He manages to make it sound like a whole orchestra. I've never played with an organ. It's so much fuller than a piano."

"Yes," agreed Ingred contemplatively.

Bess's remarks had given her an idea, but she did not want to communicate it at once to her friend. It was nothing more or less than that she should ask Dr. Linton to allow Bess to play with him some time in the Abbey. She wondered whether she dared. His temper was still decidedly irritable, and it was quite uncertain whether he would receive the suggestion graciously, or snap her head off. She thought, however, it was worth venturing.

"I'll try to catch him in an amiable mood," she decided.

In order not to arouse any grounds for irritation, she practiced particularly well, and took her next work to him at a high stage of excellence.

"Bravo!" he said, when she had finished her "Serenade." "I believe you've really got some music in you! You brought out that crescendo passage very well indeed. We want a little more delicacy in these arpeggios, and then it will do. Your touch has improved very much lately."

It was so seldom that her master launched forth into praise, that Ingred colored with pleasure. Now certainly seemed the time, if ever - to put in a word for Bess.

"Oh, Dr. Linton, may I ask you to do something for me?" she blurted out.

He thrust back his hair with a mock-pathetic gesture.

"What is it?" he inquired humorously. "Another autograph album? Or a subscription? I've grown cautious by experience, and I don't answer 'Yes, thou shalt have it to the half of my kingdom!' I never give blind promises."

"It isn't an autograph album (though I'd be glad to have your name in mine, all the same, if I may bring it some day), it is this: I've a friend at school, Bess Haselford, who plays the violin very well. She has lessons from Signor Chianti. She goes to all your recitals, and she would so *love* some time to try a piece over with the organ. Do you think, some day when you are in the Abbey, you could let her? I know it's fearful cheek to ask you!"

"Why, bring her by all means," said Dr. Linton heartily. "Let me see, I have an organ pupil to-morrow at 3.30. Suppose you come at half-past four, and I'll give her ten minutes with pleasure. I can fit it in before the choir practice, I dare say."

"Oh, thank you!" exclaimed Ingred. "We can come straight on from school."

It was delightful to have caught Dr. Linton in such an amiable mood. Ingred hastened to tell the good news to Bess, and also to beg the necessary permission from Miss Burd.

Bess, greatly thrilled, turned up next afternoon with her violin and music-case, and when classes were over they walked across to the Abbey. The pupil was just finishing his lesson, and some rather extraordinary sounds were palpitating among the arches and pillars of the old Minster.

"It must take ages to learn to manage all those stops and pedals properly," commented Bess. "I'm glad a violin has only four strings - they're quite enough!"

They sat in a pew, and waited till the lesson was over, then ventured into the chancel. Dr. Linton saw them in the looking-glass which hung over his seat, and turning round beckoned them to him.

"So you want to hear what it's like to play with an organ?" he said kindly to Bess, sounding the notes for her to tune her violin, and at the same time turning over her music. "What have we got here? It must be something I know, so that I can improvise an accompaniment. Let us try this Impromptu. Don't be afraid of your instrument, and bring the tone well out. Remember, you're in a church, and not in a drawing-room."

Bess, fluttered, nervous, but fearfully excited and pleased, declared herself ready, and launched into the Impromptu. Dr. Linton accompanied her with the finished skill of a clever musician. He subdued the organ just sufficiently to allow the violin to lead, but brought in such a beautiful range of harmonies that the piece really became a duet.

"Why, that's capital!" he declared at the conclusion. "What else have you inside that case? We'll have this Prelude now; it's rather a favorite of mine. The Bourree? Oh, we'll take that afterwards!"

Ingred had only expected Dr. Linton to play one piece with Bess, but he went on and on, and even kept the choir waiting while he made her try the Prelude over again.

"I've had quite an enjoyable half-hour," he said, shutting the books at last. "You're a sympathetic little player! Look here, the lady who was to have helped me with my recital on Sunday week has failed me. Suppose you take her place, and play the Prelude. It would go very well if we practiced it a few times together."

"Play at the recital!" gasped Bess.

"Why not? Ask your father when you go home, and send me a note to-morrow, for I want to get the thing fixed up. These boys are waiting for me now. I have to train them for an anthem. You can come and practice with me on Friday at the same time, 4.30."

Dr. Linton dismissed the girls as if he took it entirely for granted that the matter was settled. Bess was almost overwhelmed by the proposal. It was considered a great honor to play in the Abbey, and she had never dreamed that it could fall to her lot to be asked to take part in the Sunday recital. She was not sure how her father and mother would view the idea, but rather to her surprise they both readily acquiesced.

"We shall have to get your grandfather to come over and hear you," said Mr. Haselford.

"Oh yes! And may I ask Ingred to stay with us for the week-end? You see, she can't come all the way from Wynch-on-the-Wold for Sunday recitals, and it's entirely owing to her that I'm playing. I should so like her to be there."

Ingred accepted the invitation with alacrity. She had grown very fond of Bess lately - so fond, indeed, that Verity's nose was put considerably out of joint. Verity, though an amusing school comrade, was not a "home" friend. Apart from fun in their dormitory, she and Ingred had little in common, and had never arranged to spend a holiday together. She was a jolly enough girl, but so fond of "ragging" that it was impossible to do anything but joke with her. Bess, on the contrary, was a real confidante who could be trusted with secrets. The two friends spent an idyllic Saturday together. Mr. Haselford motored over to Birkshaw to fetch his father, and took the girls with him in the car. Mr. Haselford the elder proved a delightful old gentleman, deeply interested in music, and much gratified that his grand-daughter was to play at the Abbey.

"It was a happy thought of yours, my dear!" he said to Ingred. "Why, I've often attended those recitals, and never guessed little Bess would be asked to take part in one! I sang in Grovebury Abbey choir when I was a boy, and I've always had a tender spot in my heart for the old town."

"And you're not going to forget it, are you, Grandfather?" said Bess pointedly.

"Well, well, we shall see," he evaded, stroking her brown hair.

Even poor delicate Mrs. Haselford made a supreme effort and went to church on Sunday evening. It was a beautiful service, and the old Minster looked lovely with the late sunshine streaming through its gorgeous west window. Some of the congregation went away after the sermon and concluding hymn were over, but a large number stayed to hear the recital. Bess, horribly nervous, went with Ingred to the choir, where she had left her violin. There were to be two organ solos, and her piece was to separate them. She was thankful she had not to play first. She sat on one of the old carved Miserere seats, and listened as Dr. Linton's subtle fingers touched the keys, and flooded the church with the rich tones of Bach's Toccata in F Major. She wished it had been five times as long, so as to delay her own turn. But a solo cannot last for ever, and much too soon the last notes died away. There was a pause while the verger fetched a music stand and placed it close to the chancel steps. Dr. Linton was looking in her direction, and sounding the A for her. With her usually rosy face almost pale, Bess walked to the organ, tuned her violin, then took her place at the music stand. It was seldom that so young a girl had played in the Abbey, and everybody looked sympathetically at the palpably frightened little figure. It was the feeling of standing there facing all eyes that unnerved poor Bess. For a second or two her hand trembled so greatly that she could scarcely hold her bow. Then by a sudden inspiration she looked over the heads of the congregation to the west window, where the sunset light was gleaming through figures of crimson and blue and gold. Down all the centuries music had played a part in the service of the Minster. She would not remember that people were there to listen to her, but would let her violin give its praise to God alone. She did not need to look at her notes, for she knew the piece by heart, and with her eyes fixed on the west window she began the "Prelude."

Once the first notes were started, her courage returned, and she brought out her tone with a firm bow. The splendid harmonies of the organ supported her and she seemed spurred along in an impulse to do her very best. Ingred, listening in the choir, was sure her friend had never played so well, or put such depth of feeling into her music before. It was over at last, and in the hush of the church, Bess stole back to her seat, while Dr. Linton plunged into the fantasies of a "Triumphal March."

"I'm proud of you!" whispered Ingred, as they walked down the aisle together afterwards.

"Oh, don't! I felt as if it wasn't half good enough," answered Bess, giving a nervous little shiver now that the ordeal was over.

When Ingred returned to Wynch-on-the-Wold next Friday afternoon she found the family had some news for her. Old Mr. Haselford had been to Mr. Saxon's office, and had confided to him a scheme that lay very near to his heart. He had prospered exceedingly in his business affairs at Birkshaw, and he was anxious to do something for his native town of Grovebury, where he had been born and had spent his boyhood. He asked Mr. Saxon to prepare designs for a combined museum and art gallery, which he proposed to build and present to the public.

"I can trust the architect of 'Rotherwood' to give us something in the best possible taste," he had remarked. "I want the place to be an object of beauty, not the blot on the landscape that such buildings often prove. Fortunately I have the offer of a splendid site, so the plans need not be hampered by lack of space. I think we shall be able to show that the twentieth century can produce work of merit on its own lines, without slavishly copying either the classical or the mediaeval style of architecture."

Old Mr. Haselford had even gone further.

"My son's part of the business is now entirely at Grovebury," he continued. "And I feel I should like him to have a house of his own. I have bought five acres of land above the river at Trenton, on the hill, where there is a glorious view of the valley. I don't ask you to copy 'Rotherwood,' for I know no architect cares to repeat himself, but a place in the same style and with equal conveniences would suit us very well. My daughter-in-law could talk over the details. It would make a fresh interest for her. We are all tremendously keen about it."

The new schemes which occupied the minds of the Haselfords brought great rejoicings to the Bungalow.

"Why, it will almost make Father's fortune!" triumphed Ingred, still in a state of delighted bewilderment.

"It will certainly be an immense pull to him professionally to have the designing of an important public building," smiled Mother. "And I think he will be able to plan a house to satisfy Mr. and Mrs. Haselford. It's just the kind of work he likes."

"Mother, when they leave Rotherwood, shall we have to let it to any one else, or would it be possible -" Ingred hesitated, with the wish that for nearly a year she had put resolutely away from her trembling on her lips.

"To go back there ourselves?" finished Mother. "If Father's affairs prosper, as they seem likely to do at present, I think we may safely say 'yes.' It never rains but it pours, and just as his profession has suddenly taken a leap forward, his private investments have picked up. Colonial mines, that he thought

Angela Brazil

utterly done for, have begun to work again, and pay dividends. Our prospects now are very different indeed from what they were a few months ago. Don't look too excited, Ingred! Houses take a long time to build, nowadays, and it may be years before Mr. Haselford's new place is finished, and we can get re-possession of Rotherwood."

"I don't care, so long as there's hope of ever having it again!"

"It's our own home, and naturally we love it, but we must not forget what a debt of gratitude we owe to the Bungalow. We have been very happy here, and I think we have been thrown together, and have learnt to know one another in a way we should never have done at Rotherwood. All the sacrifices we have made for each other have drawn us far closer as a family, and linked us up so that we ought never to be able to drift apart now, which might have happened if we had all been able just to pursue our own line. We have learnt the value here of simple pleasures, we've enjoyed the moors and the flowers and the birds and the stars and all the beautiful things that Nature can give us. The realization of them is worth far more than anything that money can buy, for it's the 'joy that no man taketh from you.' I have grown to love Wynch-on-the-Wold so dearly that I shall beg Father to keep on the Bungalow as a country cottage, and I shall run out here for holidays when I feel Rotherwood is too much for me, and I want to be alone for a while with Nature."

"I expect we'll all want to do just the same!" said Quenrede, looking from the gay flower-beds, which her own hands had planted, over the hedge to where the brown moors stretched away into the dim gray of the distance. "I thought it was going to be hateful when I came here, but, Muvvie, I think it's been the happiest year of my life! The country may be quiet, but it has its compensation. We'll walk to the Whistling Stones again, Ingred, as soon as you break up!"

"And that will be exactly a week next Friday!" rejoiced Ingred.

The school was busy with all the usual activities that seem to happen at the end of the summer term. There was a successful cricket match with the Girls' High School from Birkshaw, a tennis tournament where Nora and Susie took part after all, and won laurels for the College, a Nature Notebook Competition in which Linda, to every one's amazement, bore off the first prize against all other schools in the town.

Then there was the annual function, when parents were invited to see a display of Swedish Drill, listen to three-part songs given by the singing class, admire the drawings and clay models exhibited in the studio, and watch a French play acted by the Sixth. It was at the close of this performance that (when friends had taken their departure, and Dr. Linton, who had conducted the singing class, had closed the grand piano and had hurried across to the Abbey to keep an appointment with an organ pupil) a certain piece of news leaked out, and began to circulate round the school. Verity had the proud importance of carrying it into the hostel.

"Do you know," she announced, "that Miss Strong is engaged to Dr. Linton, and they're to be married in the holidays?"

Nora, who was changing a crepe de chine dress for a serviceable tennis costume, collapsed on to her bed.

"Hold me up!" she murmured dramatically. "Why, I didn't know he was a widower!"

"Of course he is," endorsed Ingred, "and a most uncomfortable one, I should say. I went to his house once for a music lesson, and it looked in a fearful muddle. Good old Bantam! We must give her congrats! She'll soon get things into order there! I believe she adores little Kenneth. I've often seen her taking him about the town. She shall have my blessing, by all means!"

"We might give her something more substantial than congrats and blessings!" suggested Verity. "I vote we get up a

Angela Brazil

subscription in the form for a decent wedding present!"

"Oh yes! Think of Sarkie as Mrs. Linton! They'll be the oddest couple! I wonder if she'll get tired of perpetual music, and if he'll rage round his own drawing-room and ruffle his hair when he feels annoyed, like he does with his pupils!"

"Perhaps she'll break him off bad habits! I could trust her to hold her own."

"Oh, she'll be the gray mare, don't you fear! But honestly I'm glad! She has her points, and I hope she'll be happy."

"I wonder who'll have her form next term?"

"That doesn't concern us, for we shall probably be in the Sixth."

"Help! So we shall! I can't bring my mind to it yet. It gives me spasms!"

"Quite a blossomy prospect, though!"

On the afternoon before breaking-up day, the School Parliament met for the last time. Lispeth, rather sad, and inclined to be sentimental, reviewed from The Chair the events of the past year.

"It has been pioneer work," she said. "I dare say we might have done it better, but at least we've tried. We laid ourselves out to set a standard for the tone of the school, and I think it has kept up fairly well on the whole. The Rainbow League seems thoroughly established, and likely to go on. May I read you some of the things it has done during the year? We made four pounds for the 'War-Orphans Fund,' and sent ninety-seven home-made toys to poor children's treats. The Posy Union gave nine pots of crocuses and fifty-six bunches of flowers to cripples and invalids; the penny-a-week subscriptions have kept two little girls all the summer at the children's camp, and the Needlework Guild has made thirty-seven garments. It doesn't sound much when you put it all in hard black and white like that! I hate reports and statistics of societies, they always sound to me somehow so pharisaical, as if we were saying: 'Look how good we are!' You know I don't mean that. What I *do* mean, though, is that we've tried not to run everything entirely for ourselves. A rainbow shines when the world is clearing up, and perhaps our little efforts, small as they are, show that things are moving in the right direction. Next term all of us girls in the Sixth will have left, and a new set will take the lead. I can't say yet who will be Head of the school, but I don't fancy there's very much doubt about it. I hope whoever has the reins will keep up what we have worked so hard for this year."

Lispeth was looking straight at Ingred as she spoke; her meaning was unmistakable. Ingred blushed a faint rosy pink. It had only just dawned upon her that next term would possibly bring her the greatest honor that the College had to confer.

"Whoever is chosen for head-girl," she stammered bashfully, "I'm sure will try her very best to work for the good of the school. She couldn't do more than you've done - probably she won't do half so well - but she'll make an enormous effort to - shall we say - just 'carry on'!"

# Choose from Thousands of 1stWorldLibrary Classics By

A. M. Barnard
Ada Leverson
Adolphus William Ward
Aesop
Agatha Christie
Alexander Aaronsohn
Alexander Kielland
Alexandre Dumas
Alfred Gatty
Alfred Ollivant
Alice Duer Miller
Alice Turner Curtis
Alice Dunbar
Allen Chapman
Ambrose Bierce
Amelia E. Barr
Amory H. Bradford
Andrew Lang
Andrew McFarland Davis
Andy Adams
Anna Alice Chapin
Anna Sewell
Annie Besant
Annie Hamilton Donnell
Annie Payson Call
Annie Roe Carr
Annonaymous
Anton Chekhov
Arnold Bennett
Arthur Conan Doyle
Arthur M. Winfield
Arthur Ransome
Arthur Schnitzler
Atticus
B.H. Baden-Powell
B. M. Bower
B. C. Chatterjee
Baroness Emmuska Orczy
Baroness Orczy
Basil King
Bayard Taylor
Ben Macomber
Bertha Muzzy Bower
Bjornstjerne Bjornson
Booth Tarkington
Boyd Cable
Bram Stoker
C. Collodi
C. E. Orr

C. M. Ingleby
Carolyn Wells
Catherine Parr Traill
Charles A. Eastman
Charles Amory Beach
Charles Dickens
Charles Dudley Warner
Charles Farrar Browne
Charles Ives
Charles Kingsley
Charles Klein
Charles Hanson Towne
Charles Lathrop Pack
Charles Romyn Dake
Charles Whibley
Charles Willing Beale
Charlotte M. Braeme
Charlotte M. Yonge
Charlotte Perkins Stetson
Clair W. Hayes
Clarence Day Jr.
Clarence E. Mulford
Clemence Housman
Confucius
Coningsby Dawson
Cornelis DeWitt Wilcox
Cyril Burleigh
D. H. Lawrence
Daniel Defoe
David Garnett
Dinah Craik
Don Carlos Janes
Donald Keyhoe
Dorothy Kilner
Dougan Clark
Douglas Fairbanks
E. Nesbit
E.P.Roe
E. Phillips Oppenheim
Earl Barnes
Edgar Rice Burroughs
Edith Van Dyne
Edith Wharton
Edward Everett Hale
Edward J. O'Biren
Edward S. Ellis
Edwin L. Arnold
Eleanor Atkins
Eliot Gregory

Elizabeth Gaskell
Elizabeth McCracken
Elizabeth Von Arnim
Ellem Key
Emerson Hough
Emilie F. Carlen
Emily Dickinson
Enid Bagnold
Enilor Macartney Lane
Erasmus W. Jones
Ernie Howard Pie
Ethel May Dell
Ethel Turner
Ethel Watts Mumford
Eugenie Foa
Eugene Wood
Eustace Hale Ball
Evelyn Everett-green
Everard Cotes
F. H. Cheley
F. J. Cross
F. Marion Crawford
Federick Austin Ogg
Ferdinand Ossendowski
Francis Bacon
Francis Darwin
Frances Hodgson Burnett
Frances Parkinson Keyes
Frank Gee Patchin
Frank Harris
Frank Jewett Mather
Frank L. Packard
Frank V. Webster
Frederic Stewart Isham
Frederick Trevor Hill
Frederick Winslow Taylor
Friedrich Kerst
Friedrich Nietzsche
Fyodor Dostoyevsky
G.A. Henty
G.K. Chesterton
Gabrielle E. Jackson
Garrett P. Serviss
Gaston Leroux
George A. Warren
George Ade
Geroge Bernard Shaw
George Durston
George Ebers

George Eliot
George Gissing
George MacDonald
George Meredith
George Orwell
George Sylvester Viereck
George Tucker
George W. Cable
George Wharton James
Gertrude Atherton
Gordon Casserly
Grace E. King
Grace Gallatin
Grace Greenwood
Grant Allen
Guillermo A. Sherwell
Gulielma Zollinger
Gustav Flaubert
H. A. Cody
H. B. Irving
H.C. Bailey
H. G. Wells
H. H. Munro
H. Irving Hancock
H. Rider Haggard
H. W. C. Davis
Haldeman Julius
Hall Caine
Hamilton Wright Mabie
Hans Christian Andersen
Harold Avery
Harold McGrath
Harriet Beecher Stowe
Harry Castlemon
Harry Coghill
Harry Houidini
Hayden Carruth
Helent Hunt Jackson
Helen Nicolay
Hendrik Conscience
Hendy David Thoreau
Henri Barbusse
Henrik Ibsen
Henry Adams
Henry Ford
Henry Frost
Henry James
Henry Jones Ford
Henry Seton Merriman
Henry W Longfellow
Herbert A. Giles

Herbert Carter
Herbert N. Casson
Herman Hesse
Hildegard G. Frey
Homer
Honore De Balzac
Horace B. Day
Horace Walpole
Horatio Alger Jr.
Howard Pyle
Howard R. Garis
Hugh Lofting
Hugh Walpole
Humphry Ward
Ian Maclaren
Inez Haynes Gillmore
Irving Bacheller
Isabel Hornibrook
Israel Abrahams
Ivan Turgenev
J.G.Austin
J. Henri Fabre
J. M. Barrie
J. Macdonald Oxley
J. S. Fletcher
J. S. Knowles
J. Storer Clouston
Jack London
Jacob Abbott
James Allen
James Andrews
James Baldwin
James Branch Cabell
James DeMille
James Joyce
James Lane Allen
James Lane Allen
James Oliver Curwood
James Oppenheim
James Otis
James R. Driscoll
Jane Austen
Jane L. Stewart
Janet Aldridge
Jens Peter Jacobsen
Jerome K. Jerome
John Burroughs
John Cournos
John F. Kennedy
John Gay
John Glasworthy

John Habberton
John Joy Bell
John Kendrick Bangs
John Milton
John Philip Sousa
Jonas Lauritz Idemil Lie
Jonathan Swift
Joseph A. Altsheler
Joseph Carey
Joseph Conrad
Joseph E. Badger Jr
Joseph Hergesheimer
Joseph Jacobs
Jules Vernes
Julian Hawthrone
Julie A Lippmann
Justin Huntly McCarthy
Kakuzo Okakura
Kenneth Grahame
Kenneth McGaffey
Kate Langley Bosher
Kate Langley Bosher
Katherine Cecil Thurston
Katherine Stokes
L. A. Abbot
L. T. Meade
L. Frank Baum
Latta Griswold
Laura Dent Crane
Laura Lee Hope
Laurence Housman
Lawrence Beasley
Leo Tolstoy
Leonid Andreyev
Lewis Carroll
Lewis Sperry Chafer
Lilian Bell
Lloyd Osbourne
Louis Hughes
Louis Tracy
Louisa May Alcott
Lucy Fitch Perkins
Lucy Maud Montgomery
Luther Benson
Lydia Miller Middleton
Lyndon Orr
M. Corvus
M. H. Adams
Margaret E. Sangster
Margret Howth
Margaret Vandercook

Margret Penrose
Maria Edgeworth
Maria Thompson Daviess
Mariano Azuela
Marion Polk Angellotti
Mark Overton
Mark Twain
Mary Austin
Mary Catherine Crowley
Mary Cole
Mary Hastings Bradley
Mary Roberts Rinehart
Mary Rowlandson
M. Wollstonecraft Shelley
Maud Lindsay
Max Beerbohm
Myra Kelly
Nathaniel Hawthrone
Nicolo Machiavelli
O. F. Walton
Oscar Wilde
Owen Johnson
P.G. Wodehouse
Paul and Mabel Thorne
Paul G. Tomlinson
Paul Severing
Percy Brebner
Peter B. Kyne
Plato
R. Derby Holmes
R. L. Stevenson
R. S. Ball
Rabindranath Tagore
Rahul Alvares
Ralph Bonehill
Ralph Henry Barbour
Ralph Victor
Ralph Waldo Emmerson
Rene Descartes
Rex Beach
Rex E. Beach
Richard Harding Davis
Richard Jefferies
Richard Le Gallienne
Robert Barr
Robert Frost
Robert Gordon Anderson
Robert L. Drake
Robert Lansing
Robert Lynd
Robert Michael Ballantyne

Robert W. Chambers
Rosa Nouchette Carey
Rudyard Kipling
Samuel B. Allison
Samuel Hopkins Adams
Sarah Bernhardt
Sarah C. Hallowell
Selma Lagerlof
Sherwood Anderson
Sigmund Freud
Standish O'Grady
Stanley Weyman
Stella Benson
Stella M. Francis
Stephen Crane
Stewart Edward White
Stijn Streuvels
Swami Abhedananda
Swami Parmananda
T. S. Ackland
T. S. Arthur
The Princess Der Ling
Thomas A. Janvier
Thomas A Kempis
Thomas Anderton
Thomas Bailey Aldrich
Thomas Bulfinch
Thomas De Quincey
Thomas Dixon
Thomas H. Huxley
Thomas Hardy
Thomas More
Thornton W. Burgess
U. S. Grant
Valentine Williams
Various Authors
Vaughan Kester
Victor Appleton
Victoria Cross
Virginia Woolf
Wadsworth Camp
Walter Camp
Walter Scott
Washington Irving
Wilbur Lawton
Wilkie Collins
Willa Cather
Willard F. Baker
William Dean Howells
William le Queux
W. Makepeace Thackeray

William W. Walter
William Shakespeare
Winston Churchill
Yei Theodora Ozaki
Yogi Ramacharaka
Young E. Allison
Zane Grey